CLEOPATRA
I AM FIRE AND AIR

HAROLD BLOOM

SCRIBNER

New York   London   Toronto   Sydney   New Delhi

Scribner
An Imprint of Simon & Schuster, Inc.
1230 Avenue of the Americas
New York, NY 10020

First Scribner hardcover edition October 2017

SCRIBNER and design are registered trademarks of The Gale Group, Inc.,
used under license by Simon & Schuster, Inc., the publisher of this work.

For information about special discounts for bulk purchases,
please contact Simon & Schuster Special Sales at 1-866-506-1949
or business@simonandschuster.com.

The Simon & Schuster Speakers Bureau can bring authors to your live event.
For more information or to book an event, contact the Simon & Schuster Speakers
Bureau at 1-866-248-3049 or visit our website at www.simonspeakers.com.

Interior design by Erich Hobbing

Manufactured in the United States of America

1   3   5   7   9   10   8   6   4   2

The Library of Congress Cataloging-in-Publication Data has been applied for.

ISBN 978-1-5011-6416-3
ISBN 978-1-5011-6418-7 (ebook)

For Emily Bakemeier

Contents

Acknowledgments

I would like to acknowledge my research assistant, Alice Kenney, and my editor, Nan Graham. As always I am indebted to my literary agents, Glen Hartley and Lynn Chu. I have a particular debt to Glen Hartley, who first suggested this sequence of five brief books on Shakespeare's personalities.

Author's Note

I have tended to follow the text edited by David Bevington in the fifth edition of *The Complete Works of Shakespeare* (2004). Bevington bases his work on the *First Folio* (1623). I have repunctuated in a few places, in accordance with my understanding of the text. Sometimes I have restored Shakespeare's language, where I think traditional emendations are unfortunate.

CLEOPATRA

I AM FIRE AND AIR

CHAPTER 1

To Cool a Gipsy's Lust

I fell in love in 1974 with the Cleopatra of Janet Suzman, the South African actress who was then thirty-five. Forty-three years later her image lingers with me whenever I reread *Antony and Cleopatra*. Lithe, sinuous, agile, and exuberant, Suzman's Cleopatra is unmatched in my long years of attending performances here and in Great Britain. The ferocity of the most seductive woman in all of Shakespeare was caught in an athletic portrayal whose mood swings reflected the propulsive force of this woman's sexuality at its apex.

Antony and Cleopatra received its first performance in 1607, a year after the advent of *Macbeth*. Plutarch's account of Antony came into Shakespeare's consciousness as he overheard Macbeth's fear of Banquo being analogized to Mark Antony's eclipse by Octavius Caesar:

> To be thus is nothing, but to be safely thus:
> Our fears in Banquo stick deep,
> And in his royalty of nature reigns that
> Which would be feared. 'Tis much he dares,
> And to that dauntless temper of his mind,
> He hath a wisdom that doth guide his valour
> To act in safety. There is none but he,

Whose being I do fear; and under him
My genius is rebuked, as it is said
Mark Antony's was by Caesar.

Macbeth, act 3, scene 1, lines 47–56

The vast panoply of *Antony and Cleopatra* comprehends rather more than wanton dallying. Yet without the fierce sexuality that Cleopatra both embodies and stimulates in others, there would be no play.

After Cleopatra and her ships flee the Battle of Actium, Antony follows her. The consequence is all but total disaster. Antony's fleet is destroyed, and many of his captains desert him for Octavius Caesar. In his shame and fury, Antony chides Cleopatra and overstates her erotic career:

I found you as a morsel cold upon
Dead Caesar's trencher; nay, you were a fragment
Of Gnaeus Pompey's, besides what hotter hours,
Unregistered in vulgar fame, you have
Luxuriously picked out. For I am sure,
Though you can guess what temperance should be,
You know not what it is.

act 3, scene 13, lines 118–24

The nasty vision of Cleopatra as an Egyptian dish is augmented by Shakespeare. As he knew, she had never been the lover of Pompey the Great, who had arrived in Egypt only to be assassinated, at the command of Ptolemy XIII, one of Cleopatra's brothers. When Julius Caesar arrived in Egypt, Ptolemy XIII presented him with the head of Pompey the Great. Caesar, outraged at the affront to Roman dignity, executed the assassins. Shakespeare, taking a hint from Plutarch, has Antony add Gnaeus Pompey, Pompey the Great's son, who had visited Egypt but did not get to taste Cleopatra's electric bed.

It is important to note that the Ptolemaic dynasty, and Cleopatra as its final monarch, was a Macedonian Greek family descended from one of Alexander the Great's generals. Cleopatra was the first and only Ptolemaic ruler who spoke Egyptian as well as Greek. She saw herself as an incarnation of the goddess Isis.

Following her joint rule with her father, Ptolemy XII, and then with her brothers, Ptolemy XIII and XIV, each of whom she married, Cleopatra moved against her brothers and became the sole pharaoh, consolidating her role by an affair with Julius Caesar. Mark Antony was his successor and became the principal passion of her life, a love at once sustaining and mutually self-destructive.

These bare facts are surprisingly misleading when we confront two of Shakespeare's most exuberant personalities, Cleopatra and her Antony. Always a magpie, Shakespeare employed Plutarch and perhaps Samuel Daniel's *The Tragedy of Cleopatra* for source material. Modern historians suspect that Octavius Caesar may have executed Cleopatra, or at least induced her to suicide, which would mar and even destroy *Antony and Cleopatra*, since her exalted apotheosis of self-immolation would lose its imaginative force. Octavius executed Caesarion, whom Cleopatra bore to Julius Caesar, and Antyllus, the son of Antony by Fulvia. He did, however, spare the other children of Antony and Cleopatra.

One way to begin apprehending Cleopatra and Antony is to appreciate that they are the first celebrities in our debased sense. Charismatics, the lovers confer shreds of their glory on both their followers and their enemies. Their bounty is boundless. Antony is generous, Cleopatra something else. Hers is a giving that famishes the taker. She beguiles and she devastates.

Shakespeare follows Plutarch in showing us an Antony who is fifty-four and a Cleopatra who is thirty-nine when they first meet. Antony declines throughout the drama while Cleopatra increases in vividness and at last achieves greatness through her suicide. Poor Antony blunders and bungles. His ultimate travesty comes as he is dying and is hoisted up to the monument where Cleopatra has immured herself lest Octavius take her captive.

Somewhat departing from Plutarch, Shakespeare made Hercules rather than Bacchus or Dionysus the genius or daemon of Antony. Cleopatra's identification with the goddess Isis, whose name meant "throne," is crucial for understanding the mythic aspects of her personality. Isis gathered up the remnants of her brother and husband, Osiris, and thus aided his resurrection. The annual rising of the Nile was attributed to the tears of Isis lamenting Osiris.

Cleopatra identifies herself with the Nile and with the earth of Egypt. In her dying rapture she proclaims she is air and fire and no longer water or earth. Shakespeare's capacious imagination implies that Cleopatra as Isis marries Antony as Osiris and sustains him until his suicide. Each time I reread and teach *Antony and Cleopatra* I find myself murmuring two lines from D. H. Lawrence's poem "Don Juan":

It is Isis the mystery
Must be in love with me.

Much in Shakespeare's Cleopatra always will remain a mystery. Like Falstaff, perpetually she acts the part of herself. Theatricality is as acute in *Antony and Cleopatra* as it is in *Henry IV, Part 1* and in *Hamlet*. Cleopatra will not share the stage with anyone. Mercutio in *Romeo and Juliet* is her forerunner. Shakespeare has to kill him off before he steals the show. You cannot kill Shakespeare's Cleopatra or his Falstaff because their plays would die with them.

However equivocal Shakespeare was in regard to female sexuality, particularly in the Dark Lady Sonnets and elsewhere throughout his plays, his Cleopatra is immortal because she is the endlessly renewing fecundity of a woman's passion in the act of love. Shakespeare plays upon *will* as at once his name, sexual desire, and the male and female sexual organs, as he addresses his Cleopatra in the Dark Lady:

Whoever hath her wish, thou hast thy Will,
And Will to boot, and Will in overplus;
More than enough am I, that vex thee still,
To thy sweet will making addition thus.
Wilt thou, whose will is large and spacious,
Not once vouchsafe to hide my will in thine?
Shall will in others seem right gracious,
And in my will no fair acceptance shine?
The sea, all water, yet receives rain still,
And in abundance addeth to his store;
So thou being rich in Will, add to thy Will
One will of mine, to make thy large Will more:
    Let no unkind, no fair beseechers kill;
    Think all but one, and me in that one Will.

Sonnet 135

If thy soul check thee that I come so near,
Swear to thy blind soul that I was thy Will,

And will, thy soul knows, is admitted there;
Thus far for love, my love-suit, sweet, fulfil.
Will will fulfil the treasure of thy love,
Ay, fill it full with wills, and my will one.
In things of great receipt with ease we prove
Among a number one is reckoned none.
Then in the number let me pass untold,
Though in thy store's account I one must be.
For nothing hold me, so it please thee hold
That nothing, me, a something sweet to thee.
     Make but my name thy love, and love that still;
     And then thou lov'st me for my name is Will.

Sonnet 136

Shakespeare might well be addressing that sexual matrix, his Cleopatra. Though she has wit, canniness, political sagacity, and endless cunning, her prime attribute is astonishing sexual power. Perhaps this Cleopatra was Isis to Shakespeare's Osiris. Nowhere else, except perhaps in the Sonnets, does he yield so completely to a fascination that nevertheless frightens him. I recall again my reaction to Janet Suzman's Cleopatra, which vacillated between desire and revulsion.

Personality in Shakespeare develops rather than unfolds. Cleopatra bewilders us because she is cunning beyond male thought. She can be as witty as Falstaff, has the craftiness of Iago, as well as Hamlet's implicit ability to suggest transcendent longings. And she is irresistible.

CHAPTER 2

No Single Thing
Abides but All Things
Flow

Antony and Cleopatra is a tragicomic procession. It moves through the entire Mediterranean world from Rome to Egypt to Parthia and breathtakingly spans a decade. A bewildering profusion of short scenes enhances Shakespeare's perspectivism, the notion that what we think we see depends upon our own standpoints. Western perspectivism commences with Plato's *Protagoras* where Socrates and the Sophist Protagoras argue and each ends up with the position initially taken by the other. Emerson and Nietzsche refine perspectivism but remain inescapably Platonic.

In *Antony and Cleopatra* how you see is who you are. If you think Antony a ruffian in decline and Cleopatra an aging whore, then you know better how *you* feel but the greatness has evaded you. Should you find Antony the Herculean hero, still glorious as he wanes, and Cleopatra the sublime of erotic womanhood, burning to a final kindling, you are far closer to joining in the sad yet wonderfully comic celebration.

Shakespeare came to the composition of *Antony and Cleopatra* in the closing phase of an extraordinary fourteen months in which he wrote *King Lear*, revised it, and then descended into the night world of *Macbeth*. There is a recoiling from the terrifying inwardness of *King Lear* and of *Macbeth*, as though Shakespeare himself needed to emerge from the heart of darkness into a world of light and color. I urge you to reread *King Lear*, *Macbeth*, and *Antony and Cleopatra* in sequence, perhaps on three or four consecutive days. It is a journey from the *Inferno* to the *Purgatorio*.

No one else in Shakespeare is so metamorphic as Cleopatra. She overflows as does the Nile. Ebb, flow, return is her cycle of fecundity and renewal. Sustaining all life, Antony in particular, never tires her ebullience. Cleopatra's ardor, supremely sexual, transfigures her politically acute wisdom. She seduces world conquerors because it is her pleasure, yet also her design to preserve Egypt and her dynasty. An aura surrounds her. Gazing upon her is a transport into a radiance at once earthy and celestial. In Cleopatra Antony finds both sustenance and destruction, as his declining spirit fails to sustain her energizing glory. It is Antony's sorrow that his larger than life personality has to fade into the light of common day.

The grand set piece of *Antony and Cleopatra* is her seductive epiphany as she sails to meet Antony. Following Plutarch, Enobarbus, Antony's most devoted yet sardonic captain, describes her allure:

Enobarbus: When she first met Mark Antony, she pursed up
  his heart upon the river of Cydnus.
Agrippa: There she appeared indeed, or my reporter devised
  well for her.
Enobarbus: I will tell you.
The barge she sat in, like a burnished throne
Burned on the water. The poop was beaten gold;
Purple the sails, and so perfumèd that

The winds were love-sick with them. The oars were silver,
Which to the tune of flutes kept stroke, and made
The water which they beat to follow faster,
As amorous of their strokes. For her own person,
It beggared all description: she did lie
In her pavilion—cloth-of-gold of tissue—
O'erpicturing that Venus where we see
The fancy outwork nature. On each side her
Stood pretty dimpled boys, like smiling Cupids,
With divers-colored fans, whose wind did seem
To glow the delicate cheeks which they did cool,
And what they undid did.

Agrippa: Oh, rare for Antony!

Enobarbus: Her gentlewomen, like the Nereides,
So many mermaids, tended her i'th'eyes
And made their bends adornings. At the helm
A seeming mermaid steers. The silken tackle
Swell with the touches of those flower-soft hands,
That yarely frame the office. From the barge
A strange invisible perfume hits the sense
Of the adjacent wharfs. The city cast
Her people out upon her; and Antony,
Enthroned i'th' marketplace, did sit alone,
Whistling to th'air, which, but for vacancy,
Had gone to gaze on Cleopatra too,
And made a gap in nature.

                              act 2, scene 2, lines 195–227

Patrick Stewart, in the Trevor Nunn production enhanced by
Janet Suzman as Cleopatra, was an extraordinary Enobarbus. He

caught the contagion of the Egyptian Queen's genius for spectacle, her guarantee that her glory will be noticed and broadcast.

Agrippa: Rare Egyptian!
Enobarbus: Upon her landing, Antony sent to her,
Invited her to supper. She replied
It should be better he became her guest,
Which she entreated. Our courteous Antony,
Whom ne'er the word of 'No' woman heard speak,
Being barbered ten times o'er, goes to the feast,
And for his ordinary pays his heart
For what his eyes eat only.
Agrippa: Royal wench!
She made great Caesar lay his sword to bed;
He plowed her, and she cropped.
Enobarbus: I saw her once
Hop forty paces through the public street,
And, having lost her breath, she spoke and panted,
That she did make defect perfection,
And, breathless, power breathe forth.

act 2, scene 2, lines 227–41

The tribute is superb. Enobarbus shrewdly states Cleopatra's art that perfects her apparent aging and transmembers her breathlessness into amatory power.

Maecenas: Now Antony must leave her utterly.
Enobarbus: Never. He will not.
Age cannot wither her, nor custom stale
Her infinite variety. Other women cloy

The appetites they feed, but she makes hungry
Where most she satisfies; for vilest things
Become themselves in her, that the holy priests
Bless her when she is riggish.

act 2, scene 2, lines 242–49

Instantly putting Antony's heart in her purse, Cleopatra directs and enacts an erotic spectacle in which her barge becomes a lustrous throne burning on the water. Purple and gold and silver shine vividly and the perfumed sails intoxicate winds until they are sick with love. Lascivious melodies from flutes keep amorous strokes and work upon the water as aphrodisiacs. Cleopatra herself reclines invitingly, a silky and golden Venus, surrounded by Cupids with multicolored fans cooling yet rendering incandescent the cheeks of the wanton Queen.

Mermaidlike and responsive to every glance of their mistress, her women bow to her with voluptuous grace. Overcome with desire, Agrippa, who is Octavius Caesar's henchman, salutes her as a truly royal wench who bedded Julius Caesar and gave birth to his son Caesarion. Enobarbus is marvelous in his responses. The middle-aged Cleopatra, hopping through the streets of Alexandria, makes of her breathlessness another sign of sexual dynamism.

The ultimate tribute of Enobarbus is the famous: "Age cannot wither her, nor custom stale / Her infinite variety." Radiant at thirty-nine, Cleopatra offers a sexual fulfillment that changes with each coupling. Where other women glut their lovers' appetites, Cleopatra alone overwhelmingly satisfies yet stimulates fresh desire. Most outrageously and joyously, the priests of Isis bless her when she is surpassingly lustful. Even the vilest practices are becoming when they are hers: "for vilest things / Become themselves in her." "Become" is the refrain heard throughout this great pageant. There are seventeen instances in *Antony and Cleopatra* of the word "become" and its variations. I recall only one "became" in all of *Hamlet*, which is a drama of being and unbeing. Cleopatra's play centers upon becoming.

What shall we call the mutual love of Cleopatra and Antony? In the first and in the last place it is sexual. The two supreme narcissists behold themselves more radiantly in the eyes of the other. Yet they are not equals. Antony submits incessantly but Cleopatra will not yield to the flux of time. Shakespeare subtly hints that Antony props himself upon Cleopatra in order to find sustenance for his wavering spirit. Yet not even her endlessly burgeoning vitality can prevent his fall.

Shakespeare was a master of ellipsis, of leaving things out so as to stimulate our curiosity as to origins. Except for a brief moment in the wings when Antony curses her treachery, we never see him and Cleopatra alone together. When not coupling, how are they with each other? Cleopatra mentions one occasion when they changed gender roles. She attired him in her garments and put on his armor to wield his favorite sword, Philippi, with which he defeated the forces of Cassius and Brutus.

It is difficult to visualize a mutual solitude for these two fierce individualities. They depend upon the basking of their followers. In them Shakespeare invented a new kind of charismatic, in which adulation is essential for the bliss of supremacy.

CHAPTER 3

O'erflows the Measure

Antony and Cleopatra begins with Philo, one of Antony's officers, lamenting to another the foolish infatuation of their commander:

Nay, but this dotage of our general's
O'erflows the measure. Those his goodly eyes,
That o'er the files and musters of the war
Have glowed like plated Mars, now bend, now turn
The office and devotion of their view
Upon a tawny front. His captain's heart,
Which in the scuffles of great fights hath burst
The buckles on his breast, reneges all temper
And is become the bellows and the fan
To cool a gipsy's lust. Look, where they come.
Take but good note, and you shall see in him
The triple pillar of the world transformed
Into a strumpet's fool. Behold and see.

act 1, scene 1, lines 1–13

Everything in this great drama "o'erflows the measure." The Nile rises, floods its banks, brings abundance to the land of Egypt. Antony's and Cleopatra's titanic personalities break down all limits:

Cleopatra: If it be love indeed, tell me how much.

Antony: There's beggary in the love that can be reckoned.

Cleopatra: I'll set a bourn how far to be beloved.

Antony: Then must thou needs find out new heaven, new earth.

act 1, scene 1, lines 14–17

Flirtatiously Cleopatra teases Antony by threatening to set a boundary to his passion. In the accents of Revelation he vaunts that a new heaven and a new earth will have to be discovered by the charmer he calls: "my serpent of old Nile." Refusing to hear ambassadors sent by Rome he cries out:

> Let Rome in Tiber melt and the wide arch
> Of the ranged empire fall! Here is my space.
> Kingdoms are clay; our dungy earth alike
> Feeds beast as man. The nobleness of life
> Is to do thus; when such a mutual pair
> And such a twain can do't, in which I bind,
> On pain of punishment, the world to weet
> We stand up peerless.

act 1, scene 1, lines 35–42

This might be called the epiphany of their passion and of their pride. Antony means it and does not mean it. He covets Rome and Egypt. He wants the entire world. The grandeur of his history culminates in the fierce embrace enjoyed with Cleopatra. Explicitly he lauds the sexual merging of himself as Hercules and Cleopatra as Isis. They are a twain unparalleled upon whom the world must render the judgment of peerlessness.

Pride in their mutual prowess—political, military, lovemaking—

is a principal constituent of their glory. This pride is akin to Falstaff's delight in his own language, and to Hamlet's trust in the reach of his consciousness.

You might say that the world is the third major personality in *Antony and Cleopatra*. Octavius Caesar, the future first emperor as Augustus, pales in the presence of Cleopatra, her Antony, and the wide world. Octavius will destroy Cleopatra and Antony and become the universal landlord who imposes a Roman peace. And yet even he, and the world, become audience for the imperial lovers who take the stage away and make it their own:

Cleopatra: Excellent falsehood!
Why did he marry Fulvia, and not love her?
I'll seem the fool I am not. Antony
Will be himself.
Antony: But stirred by Cleopatra.
Now, for the love of Love and her soft hours,
Let's not confound the time with conference harsh.
There's not a minute of our lives should stretch
Without some pleasure now. What sport tonight?
Cleopatra: Hear the ambassadors.
Antony: Fie, wrangling queen!
Whom everything becomes—to chide, to laugh,
To weep; whose every passion fully strives
To make itself, in thee, fair and admired!
No messenger but thine; and all alone
Tonight we'll wander through the streets and note
The qualities of people. Come, my queen,
Last night you did desire it.—Speak not to us.

                                        act 1, scene 1, lines 42–57

15

Taunting her lover, Cleopatra reminds him of his warlike wife, Fulvia, whom he does not love. She shrugs herself off, saying she prefers to believe him, when he says only pleasure matters, though she knows otherwise. His infatuated response turns upon the rich word "stirred," which compounds sexual arousal, folly, and stimulation to noble exploits. "Whom everything becomes—to chide, to laugh, / To weep." "Becomes" sounds again as if to remind us of Cleopatra's ebb and flow, like her Nile. Antony chooses prolongation of delights, prompted by forebodings of an end to come. Deftly Cleopatra evades him and demands that he hear the ambassadors.

There is a rush to bright destruction as Antony admires the passion of his Isis. Unknowingly he speaks as Osiris, blind to his own scattering and enchanted by a goddess whose tears and laughter alike enhance her beauty.

Ebb and flow, the rhythm of time's river, soon enough brings Roman Antony to hear the resonance of the opposite:

Enobarbus: Hush! Here comes Antony.
Charmian: Not he. The Queen.
Cleopatra: Saw you my lord?
Enobarbus: No, lady.
Cleopatra: Was he not here?
Charmian: No, madam.
Cleopatra: He was disposed to mirth, but on the sudden
A Roman thought hath struck him. Enobarbus!

act 1, scene 2, lines 73–80

Cleopatra shrewdly intuits that "a Roman thought" will take Antony away from her. Politics and passion fuse in her realization.

Enobarbus: Madam?

Cleopatra: Seek him and bring him hither. Where's Alexas?

Alexas: Here, at your service.—My lord approaches.

Cleopatra: We will not look upon him. Go with us.

act 1, scene 2, lines 81–84

Her disdain is both authentic and tactical, reminding us that while she perpetually acts the part of herself, she is aware of the limits of the histrionic. The messenger reports that Antony's wife, Fulvia, and his brother, Lucius, were defeated by Octavian. Bad news multiplies. The Parthians have broken through Roman lines. Fulvia has died. Antony, who did not love her, praises her as a great spirit gone. A new awareness warns him he must break his Egyptian fetters and abandon the "enchanting Queen":

Antony: How now, Enobarbus!

Enobarbus: What's your pleasure, sir?

Antony: I must with haste from hence.

Enobarbus: Why, then, we kill all our women. We see how
mortal an unkindness is to them; if they suffer our
departure, death's the word.

Antony: I must be gone.

Enobarbus: Under a compelling occasion, let women die. It
were pity to cast them away for nothing, though between
them and a great cause they should be esteemed nothing.
Cleopatra, catching but the least noise of this, dies
instantly; I have seen her die twenty times upon far poorer
moment. I do think there is mettle in death which commits
some loving act upon her, she hath such a celerity in dying.

act 1, scene 2, lines 129–42

Enobarbus is meticulous in describing Cleopatra's passionate genius at mock dying, a crucial weapon in her arsenal.

> **Antony:** She is cunning past man's thought.
> **Enobarbus:** Alack, sir, no, her passions are made of nothing
> but the finest part of pure love. We cannot call her
> winds and waters sighs and tears; they are greater storms
> and tempests than almanacs can report. This cannot be
> cunning in her; if it be, she makes a shower of rain as
> well as Jove.
> **Antony:** Would I had never seen her!
> **Enobarbus:** Oh, sir, you had then left unseen a wonderful
> piece of work, which not to have been blessed withal
> would have discredited your travel.
>
> > act 1, scene 2, lines 143–52

The language is admirable and comic, telling us again that *Antony and Cleopatra* cannot be subsumed by genre or categories. Poor Antony, enthralled by her, at once admires her art and ruefully is reduced to wishing their relationship undone. The diction of Enobarbus triumphs as he echoes Hamlet.

> What piece of work is a man—how noble in reason;
> how infinite in faculties, in form and moving; how
> express and admirable in action; how like an angel in
> apprehension; how like a god;
>
> > *Hamlet*, act 2, scene 2, lines 269–72

Cleopatra is a piece of work wonderful in another mode, erotic and yet transcendent.

Antony: Fulvia is dead.

Enobarbus: Sir?

Antony: Fulvia is dead.

Enobarbus: Fulvia?

Antony: Dead.

Enobarbus: Why, sir, give the gods a thankful sacrifice. When
it pleaseth their deities to take the wife of a man from
him, it shows to man the tailors of the earth; comforting
therein, that when old robes are worn out, there are
members to make new. If there were no more women
but Fulvia, then had you indeed a cut, and the case to be
lamented. This grief is crowned with consolation; your
old smock brings forth a new petticoat, and indeed the
tears live in an onion that should water this sorrow.

act 1, scene 2, lines 153–66

This is captivating, as though Enobarbus has caught the contagion of Falstaff's joyous wit, and makes me wish Shakespeare had
augmented this role.

Antony: The business she hath broachèd in the state
Cannot endure my absence.

Enobarbus: And the business you have broached here cannot
be without you, especially that of Cleopatra's, which
wholly depends on your abode.

Antony: No more light answers. Let our officers
Have notice what we purpose. I shall break
The cause of our expedience to the Queen
And get her leave to part.

. . .

> Say our pleasure,
> To such whose place is under us, requires
> Our quick remove from hence.
> **Enobarbus:** I shall do't.

act 1, scene 2, lines 167–92

This sequence is essential to apprehending the renewed surge of Antony's dynamism. Suddenly Roman, he desires facts and not illusions. His Herculean winds of potency rise and he accepts hearing his faults as an improvement, a plowing that will root out his errors and restore his sense of the ground of his glory.

The wheel of Fortune and of time sinking warns Antony that his pleasure will lead to chagrin. The laughing cynic Enobarbus plays upon a woman dying as her achievement of orgasm. Cleopatra frequently feigns death, dramatically fainting when it suits her, so that her deaths involve an augmentation of "mettle" or sexual exuberance. We like Enobarbus for his outspoken honesty, his devotion to Antony, and his bawdy wit. But Antony is again a Roman political general and brushes aside these light answers. His martial spirit overflows the measure and he reassumes Herculean stature.

CHAPTER 4

Oh, My Oblivion
Is a Very Antony

Cleopatra's histrionic suppleness is lithe and luminous as she enters the agon with Antony's Roman thoughts. Her language dances and darts like a swallow from mood to mood. Roman thoughts are brutal. Violence, financial corruption, cupidity, and the arrogance of a masculine pride rampant are the grounds of Roman authority. All of them—Pompey the Great, Julius Caesar, Mark Antony, Octavius Caesar—augment the foundations of Rome with rivers of blood. Shakespeare avoids moral judgment, as always, but what audience would not prefer Cleopatra's quicksilver strategies of political and erotic wit?

Cleopatra: Where is he?
Charmian: I did not see him since.
Cleopatra: [*to Alexas*] See where he is, who's with him, what
    he does.
I did not send you. If you find him sad,
Say I am dancing; if in mirth, report
That I am sudden sick. Quick, and return.   [*Exit Alexas*]
Charmian: Madam, methinks if you did love him dearly,

You do not hold the method to enforce
The like from him.

Cleopatra: What should I do I do not?

Charmian: In each thing give him way; cross him in nothing.

Cleopatra: Thou teachest like a fool: the way to lose him.

Charmian: Tempt him not so too far. I wish, forbear;
In time we hate that which we often fear.
But here comes Antony.

Cleopatra: I am sick and sullen.

act 1, scene 3, lines 1–13

She is and she is not. Can so great an actress always know when she is or is not acting? The law of Cleopatra's personality is ebb, flow, ebb, return. Each return is a renewal and vitalizes afresh. Antony's personality is ebb, flow, ebb, and do not return. His is the way down and out.

Antony: I am sorry to give breathing to my purpose—

Cleopatra: Help me away, dear Charmian! I shall fall.
It cannot be thus long; the sides of nature
Will not sustain it.

Antony: Now, my dearest queen—

Cleopatra: Pray you, stand further from me.

Antony: What's the matter?

Cleopatra: I know by that same eye there's some good news.
What says the married woman you may go?
Would she had never given you leave to come!
Let her not say 'tis I that keep you here.
I have no power upon you; hers you are.

Antony: The gods best know—

Cleopatra: O, never was there queen
So mightily betrayed! Yet at the first
I saw the treasons planted.
Antony: Cleopatra—
Cleopatra: Why should I think you can be mine, and true—
Though you in swearing shake the thronèd gods—
Who have been false to Fulvia? Riotous madness,
To be entangled with those mouth-made vows
Which break themselves in swearing!
Antony: Most sweet queen—
Cleopatra: Nay, pray you, seek no color for your going,
But bid farewell and go. When you sued staying,
Then was the time for words. No going then.
Eternity was in our lips and eyes,
Bliss in our brows' bent; none our parts so poor,
But was a race of heaven. They are so still,
Or thou, the greatest soldier of the world,
Art turned the greatest liar.

                    act 1, scene 3, lines 14–39

She is sublime and irrefutable. There is massive dignity in her: "They are so still." Antony, indubitably the greatest soldier of the world, is neither a common liar nor the greatest liar. He has no skill in prevarication. Confronted by her variety, he is dumbfounded.

The startled Antony provokes one of her finest declarations:

Antony: How now, lady?
Cleopatra: I would I had thy inches. Thou shouldst know
There were a heart in Egypt.

                    act 1, scene 3, lines 39–41

This phallic tribute is accompanied by the earned pride of Cleopatra or Egypt in her indubitable courage. What quiets her is Antony's pledge made remarkable by his trope assuming the role of Osiris, whose father was the sun: "By the fire / That quickens Nilus' slime, I go from hence / Thy soldier" (act 1, scene 3, lines 68–70). The supposedly fainting Cleopatra cannot cease provoking her Osiris:

Cleopatra: Cut my lace, Charmian, come!
But let it be; I am quickly ill, and well,
So Antony loves.
Antony: My precious queen, forbear,
And give true evidence to his love which stands
An honorable trial.
Cleopatra: So Fulvia told me.
I prithee, turn aside and weep for her;
Then bid adieu to me, and say the tears
Belong to Egypt. Good now, play one scene
Of excellent dissembling, and let it look
Like perfect honor.
Antony: You'll heat my blood. No more.
Cleopatra: You can do better yet; but this is meetly.
Antony: Now, by my sword—
Cleopatra: And target. Still he mends.
But this is not the best. Look, prithee, Charmian,
How this Herculean Roman does become
The carriage of his chafe.
Antony: I'll leave you, lady.
Cleopatra: Courteous lord, one word.
Sir, you and I must part, but that's not it;

Sir, you and I have loved, but there's not it;
That you know well. Something it is I would—
Oh, my oblivion is a very Antony,
And I am all forgotten.

act 1, scene 3, lines 71–92

This moment, in a play of endless wonders, stands out for its transition from Cleopatra's theatricality to her all-too-human shock at what is happening to threaten her joy. "How this Herculean Roman does become / The carriage of his chafe" again invokes "become" to her dismay. For once her wit fails and she reaches for what she cannot find. There is a world of cognitive music in her bewilderment:

Oh, my oblivion is a very Antony,
And I am all forgotten.

"Oblivion" is a rich word here, since her momentary confusion is primal and passionate. Performative art abandons her and a woman in love dreading loss scarcely seems Cleopatra of Egypt. She forgets herself and is flooded by the anxiety that he may forget her. An uncharacteristic stasis dominates, as Shakespeare moves on to the great world in contention.

After an interlude with Octavius Caesar censuring Antony for his lascivious carousals in Alexandria, the future Augustus is alarmed by the threat of the younger Pompey and his piratical followers. Suddenly needing Antony's generalship and his troops, the politic Octavius cries out for the Herculean hero to return to himself. We bear this as best we can, since this bureaucrat is hard to enjoy.

Life flows back with the bereft Cleopatra surmising the present state of her absent lover:

> Oh, Charmian,
> Where think'st thou he is now? Stands he or sits he?
> Or does he walk? or is he on his horse?
> Oh, happy horse, to bear the weight of Antony!
> Do bravely, horse, for wot'st thou whom thou mov'st?
> The demi-Atlas of this earth, the arm
> And burgonet of men.
>
> act 1, scene 5, lines 19–25

"Do" carries sexual implication. Antony holds up half the earth and is the arm and steel helmet of mankind. The metric moves erotically, the questions and exclamations set up a rhythm of exultant longing. In that coursing we meditate on the whole Cleopatra and find that she is endless. Like Falstaff and Hamlet, and like Shakespeare, her capaciousness is infinite. Like Juliet, her love is like the bounty of the sea. The more she gives, the more she has. We neither admire her nor find her repellent. Her peregrine spirit quests beyond our intense feeling with and for her. Vistas to which we cannot stretch forth our hands abide with her on a farther shore.

> He's speaking now,
> Or murmuring, 'Where's my serpent of old Nile?'
> For so he calls me. Now I feed myself
> With most delicious poison. Think on me,
> That am with Phoebus' amorous pinches black
> And wrinkled deep in time. Broad-fronted Caesar,

When thou wast here above the ground, I was
A morsel for a monarch. And great Pompey
Would stand and make his eyes grow in my brow;
There would he anchor his aspect, and die
With looking on his life.

act 1, scene 5, lines 25–35

Her sexual longing identifies her with Antony's steed and the "most delicious poison" presages the manner of her dying. A curious realism informs her sense of her dark coloring, burned by the sun of Egypt, and of her aging toward meridian. Recollections of Julius Caesar and of Pompey the Great (Shakespeare's departure from history) bring back her pride.

She surges into an ecstasy that sets Antony above Julius Caesar:

Cleopatra: Did I, Charmian,
Ever love Caesar so?
Charmian: Oh, that brave Caesar!
Cleopatra: Be choked with such another emphasis!
Say, 'the brave Antony.'
Charmian: The valiant Caesar!
Cleopatra: By Isis, I will give thee bloody teeth
If thou with Caesar paragon again
My man of men.
Charmian: By your most gracious pardon,
I sing but after you.
Cleopatra: My salad days,
When I was green in judgment, cold in blood,
To say as I said then. But, come, away,
Get me ink and paper.

He shall have every day a several greeting,
Or I'll unpeople Egypt.

act 1, scene 5, lines 69–81

It has become too familiar: "My salad days, / When I was green in judgment." In this play it evokes nostalgia for what was, for what is, and what soon must pass into oblivion.

CHAPTER 5

Antony and Octavia:
A Sacrifice to Roman Power

Because Octavius and Antony need to ally against the younger Pompey and his mastery of the sea, they make a pact by which Octavia, the sister of Octavius Caesar, and Mark Antony marry each other. She is reduced to an unhappy expedient. Uneasy always in the presence of Octavius, Antony has his forebodings confirmed by an uncannily accurate soothsayer:

Antony: Now, sirrah: you do wish yourself in Egypt?
Soothsayer: Would I had never come from thence, nor you
    thither!
Antony: If you can, your reason?
Soothsayer: I see it in my motion, have it not in my tongue;
But yet hie you to Egypt again.
Antony: Say to me, whose fortunes shall
    rise higher,
Caesar's or mine?
Soothsayer: Caesar's.
Therefore, O Antony, stay not by his side.
Thy daemon—that thy spirit which keeps thee—is
Noble, courageous, high, unmatchable,

Where Caesar's is not; but, near him, thy angel
Becomes afeard, as being o'erpowered. Therefore
Make space enough between you.
Antony: Speak this no more.

act 2, scene 3, lines 10–24

"But, near him, thy angel / Becomes afeard, as being o'erpowered" plays again upon "becoming." Antony recognizes the menace. His vitality diminishes in the presence of Octavius Caesar. A personality so magnetic and exuberant cannot compete with a colorless but oncoming presage of future empire.

Soothsayer: To none but thee; no more but when to thee.
If thou dost play with him at any game,
Thou art sure to lose; and of that natural luck
He beats thee 'gainst the odds. Thy luster thickens
When he shines by. I say again, thy spirit
Is all afraid to govern thee near him;
But, he away, 'tis noble.
Antony: Get thee gone.
Say to Ventidius I would speak with him.

                                        [*Exit (Soothsayer)*]

He shall to Parthia.—Be it art or hap,
He hath spoken true. The very dice obey him,
And in our sports my better cunning faints
Under his chance. If we draw lots, he speeds;
His cocks do win the battle still of mine
When it is all to naught, and his quails ever
Beat mine, inhooped, at odds. I will to Egypt;

And though I make this marriage for my peace,
I'th'East my pleasure lies.

act 2, scene 3, lines 25–41

Antony's language hesitates and stumbles. He is mystified yet convinced that his genius wanes in competition with Octavius. We could not conceive that Cleopatra ever might fear the power of another woman.

Roman behavior has to be heartless. It measures men and women as means to the end of accumulating power. Octavius professes love for his sister yet exploits her for his Machiavellian purposes. Antony, sublime hedonist, plays politics with this dubious marriage and lusts for Cleopatra.

Directly before the ominous soothsaying, Shakespeare places the farewell of the newly married couple:

Antony: The world and my great office will sometimes
Divide me from your bosom.
Octavia: All which time
Before the gods my knee shall bow my prayers
To them for you.
Antony: Good night, sir. My Octavia,
Read not my blemishes in the world's report.
I have not kept my square, but that to come
Shall all be done by th'rule. Good night, dear lady.
Good night, sir.
Octavius: Good night.

act 2, scene 3, lines 1–9

This is another phase of Antony's long decline. He does not mean what he says and we know it. And yet there is always a touch of compassionate grandeur:

Antony: No further, sir.
Octavius: You take from me a great part of myself;
Use me well in't.—Sister, prove such a wife
As my thoughts make thee, and as my farthest bond
Shall pass on thy approof.—Most noble Antony,
Let not the piece of virtue, which is set
Betwixt us as the cement of our love
To keep it builded, be the ram to batter
The fortress of it; for better might we
Have loved without this mean, if on both parts
This be not cherished.
Antony:　　　　　　Make me not offended
In your distrust.
Octavius:　　　I have said.
Antony:　　　　　　　You shall not find,
Though you be therein curious, the least cause
For what you seem to fear.

　　　　　　　　　　act 3, scene 2, lines 23–36

Octavius is grim and accurately suspicious. Antony embraces the lie. You cannot choose between them in terms of morality. They have none. But Antony wins us perpetually because he is large. A lost grandeur makes him a noble ruin, not of Cleopatra but of his own designing.

Antony: So the gods keep you,

And make the hearts of Romans serve your ends!

We will here part.

Octavius: Farewell, my dearest sister, fare thee well.

The elements be kind to thee, and make

Thy spirits all of comfort! Fare thee well.

Octavia: [*weeping*] My noble brother!

Antony: The April's in her eyes; it is love's spring,

And these the showers to bring it on.—Be cheerful.

Octavia: [*to Octavius*] Sir, look well to my husband's house;

       and—

Octavius: What, Octavia?

Octavia: I'll tell you in your ear. [*She whispers*]

Antony: Her tongue will not obey her heart, nor can

Her heart inform her tongue—the swan's down feather,

That stands upon the swell at full of tide,

And neither way inclines.

                                   act 3, scene 2, lines 36–50

With all his hypocrisy in this marriage, we along with Antony are touched by his perceptiveness. Antony's sorrow is real enough but hollow. Too torn to speak aloud, Octavia in Antony's eyes becomes the feather of a swan that floats at full tide and can move neither up nor downstream. Octavius fights to hold back tears, doubtless for outward show, and Antony embraces him in a false farewell. Enobarbus the ironist deprecates both the sorrow of Octavius and the tears Antony summoned at the deaths of Julius Caesar and of Brutus.

Enobarbus: [*aside to Agrippa*] Will Caesar weep?

Agrippa: [*aside to Enobarbus*] He has a cloud in's face.

Enobarbus: [*aside to Agrippa*] He were the worse for that, were
    he a horse;

So is he, being a man.

Agrippa: [*aside to Enobarbus*] Why, Enobarbus,

When Antony found Julius Caesar dead,

He cried almost to roaring; and he wept

When at Philippi he found Brutus slain.

Enobarbus: [*aside to Agrippa*] That year indeed he was
    troubled with a rheum.

What willingly he did confound he wailed,

Believe't, till I wept too.

act 3, scene 2, lines 51–59

We will see Octavia only twice after this. She is pathetic when
Antony in Athens rids himself of her by sending her back to her
brother. Returning to Rome the pathos augments, accompanied by
the fury of Octavius Caesar:

Octavius: No, my most wrongèd sister. Cleopatra

Hath nodded him to her. He hath given his empire

Up to a whore, who now are levying

The kings o'th'earth for war. He hath assembled

Bocchus, the King of Libya; Archelaus,

Of Cappadocia; Philadelphos, King

Of Paphlagonia; the Thracian king, Adallas;

King Malchus of Arabia; King of Pont;

Herod of Jewry; Mithridates, King

Of Comagene; Polemon and Amyntas,

34

The Kings of Mede and Lycaonia,
With a more larger list of scepters.
Octavia: Ay me, most wretched,
That have my heart parted betwixt two friends
That do afflict each other!
Octavius: Welcome hither.
Your letters did withhold our breaking forth
Till we perceived both how you were wrong led
And we in negligent danger.

act 3, scene 6, lines 67–84

The true accent of Octavius is heard in the cold comfort he offers to Octavia:

                    Cheer your heart.
Be you not troubled with the time, which drives
O'er your content these strong necessities,
But let determined things to destiny
Hold unbewailed their way.

act 3, scene 2, lines 84–88

The Roman victor rings in those phrases. He cheers only his own heart with the prospect of a total triumph. Our pleasure is in the East with Cleopatra, whose personality now expands in a continuous crescendo.

CHAPTER 6

I That Do Bring
the News Made Not
the Match

Antony and Cleopatra is a brilliant kaleidoscope, a montage of shifting fortunes, places, personalities, excursions into the empyrean. The Serpent of Old Nile returns in two scenes that Shakespeare subtly divides, in which Cleopatra receives with fury the news of Antony's remarriage and then turns her cunning to meet the crisis:

[*Enter a Messenger*]
Cleopatra: Oh, from Italy!
Ram thou thy fruitful tidings in mine ears,
That long time have been barren.
Messenger: Madam, madam—
Cleopatra: Antonio's dead! If thou say so, villain,
Thou kill'st thy mistress; but well and free,
If thou so yield him, there is gold, and here
My bluest veins to kiss—a hand that kings
Have lipped, and trembled kissing.
              [*She offers him gold, and her hand to kiss*]
Messenger: First, madam, he is well.

Cleopatra: Why, there's more gold. But sirrah, mark, we use
To say the dead are well. Bring it to that,
The gold I give thee will I melt and pour
Down thy ill-uttering throat.

act 2, scene 5, lines 23–35

Antony and Cleopatra, doubtless because of its vastness and space and length of time, depends upon messengers. Breaking bad news to Cleopatra is a very dangerous occupation. She is perfectly capable of pouring molten gold down the unhappy messenger's throat.

Messenger: Good madam, hear me.
Cleopatra: Well, go to, I will.
But there's no goodness in thy face, if Antony
Be free and healthful—so tart a favor
To trumpet such good tidings! If not well,
Thou shouldst come like a Fury crowned with snakes,
Not like a formal man.
Messenger: Will't please you hear me?
Cleopatra: I have a mind to strike thee ere thou speak'st.

act 2, scene 5, lines 36–43

That monitory blow would be the least the unfortunate messenger should fear. To punish in advance has a sadistic element, yet that is a component in Cleopatra's sexual ferocity.

Cleopatra: Yet if thou say Antony lives, is well,
Or friends with Caesar, or not captive to him,
I'll set thee in a shower of gold and hail

Rich pearls upon thee.

Messenger: Madam, he's well.

Cleopatra: Well said.

Messenger: And friends with Caesar.

Cleopatra: Thou'rt an honest man.

Messenger: Caesar and he are greater friends than ever.

Cleopatra: Make thee a fortune from me.

Messenger: But yet, madam—

Cleopatra: I do not like 'But yet'; it does allay

The good precedence. Fie upon 'But yet'!

'But yet' is as a jailer to bring forth

Some monstrous malefactor. Prithee, friend,

Pour out the pack of matter to mine ear,

The good and bad together. He's friends with Caesar,

In state of health, thou say'st, and, thou sayst, free.

Messenger: Free, madam? No, I made no such report.

He's bound unto Octavia.

Cleopatra: For what good turn?

Messenger: For the best turn i'th' bed.

                              act 2, scene 5, lines 44–60

Blurting out the truth, he risks his life, and probably knows it.

Cleopatra: I am pale, Charmian.

Messenger: Madam, he's married to Octavia.

Cleopatra: The most infectious pestilence upon thee!

                              [*Strikes him down*]

Messenger: Good madam, patience.

Cleopatra: What say you? [*Strikes him*]

                              Hence,

Horrible villain, or I'll spurn thine eyes
Like balls before me! I'll unhair thy head!

[*She hales him up and down*]

Thou shalt be whipped with wire and stewed in brine,
Smarting in ling'ring pickle!
Messenger: Gracious madam,
I that do bring the news made not the match.

act 2, scene 5, lines 60–68

To call this Cleopatra a hellcat seems an understatement. After striking the unhappy Messenger twice, she drags him up and down and is about to knife him when off he runs. Sagacity returns with the realization that she has loved too well. Feigning a collapse she yet confronts her own ambivalence at being abandoned. Her Antony is now a perspective, Gorgon one way, Mars the other. Curiously, she sees him as the female Gorgon, serpentine and turning victims to stone. Yet her discomfiture passes into a cold estimate of her rival.

When again we are in her Alexandrian palace, the wretched Messenger is called back and saves himself from another beating with his apt responses:

Cleopatra: Where is the fellow?
Alexas: Half afeard to come.
Cleopatra: Go to, go to.   [*Enter the Messenger as before*]
                    Come hither, sir.
Alexas: Good Majesty,
Herod of Jewry dare not look upon you
But when you are well pleased.
Cleopatra: That Herod's head

I'll have; but how, when Antony is gone,

Through whom I might command it?—Come thou near.

Messenger: Most gracious Majesty!

Cleopatra: Didst thou behold Octavia?

Messenger: Ay, dread Queen.

Cleopatra: Where?

Messenger: Madam, in Rome.

I looked her in the face, and saw her led

Between her brother and Mark Antony.

Cleopatra: Is she as tall as me?

Messenger: She is not, madam.

Cleopatra: Didst hear her speak? Is she shrill-tongued or low?

Messenger: Madam, I heard her speak. She is low-voiced.

Cleopatra: That's not so good. He cannot like her long.

Charmian: Like her! Oh, Isis, 'tis impossible.

Cleopatra: I think so, Charmian. Dull of tongue, and dwarfish.—

What majesty is in her gait? Remember,

If e'er thou looked'st on majesty.

Messenger: She creeps:

Her motion and her station are as one.

She shows a body rather than a life,

A statue than a breather.

Cleopatra: Is this certain?

Messenger: Or I have no observance.

Charmian: Three in Egypt

Cannot make better note.

Cleopatra: He's very knowing,

I do perceive't. There's nothing in her yet.

The fellow has good judgment.

Charmian: Excellent.

Cleopatra: Guess at her years, I prithee.

Messenger: Madam,

She was a widow—

Cleopatra: Widow? Charmian, hark.

Messenger: And I do think she's thirty.

Cleopatra: Bear'st thou her face in mind? Is't long or round?

Messenger: Round, even to faultiness.

Cleopatra: For the most part, too, they are foolish that are

so.—

Her hair, what color?

Messenger: Brown, madam; and her forehead

As low as she would wish it.

Cleopatra: [*giving money*] There's gold for thee.

Thou must not take my former sharpness ill.

I will employ thee back again; I find thee

Most fit for business. Go make thee ready;

Our letters are prepared. [*Exit Messenger*]

Charmian: A proper man.

Cleopatra: Indeed, he is so. I repent me much

That so I harried him. Why, methinks, by him,

This creature's no such thing.

Charmian: Nothing, madam.

Cleopatra: The man hath seen some majesty, and should know.

act 3, scene 3, lines 1–45

This intricate dance of dispraise rescues the Messenger and restores Cleopatra's pride in her own sexual allure. She knows as we do that Antony must return to her strong toil of grace.

CHAPTER 7

In the East
My Pleasure Lies

Shakespeare chooses not to show us the reunion of Cleopatra and Antony. Perhaps he feared one climax after another in this flowing cavalcade. We learn of their reconciliation only from Octavius:

Octavius: Contemning Rome, he has done all this and more
In Alexandria. Here's the manner of 't:
I'th' marketplace, on a tribunal silvered,
Cleopatra and himself in chairs of gold
Were publicly enthroned. At the feet sat
Caesarion, whom they call my father's son,
And all the unlawful issue that their lust
Since then hath made between them. Unto her
He gave the stablishment of Egypt, made her
Of lower Syria, Cyprus, Lydia,
Absolute queen.
Maecenas: This in the public eye?
Octavius: I'th' common showplace, where they exercise.
His sons he there proclaimed the kings of kings:
Great Media, Parthia, and Armenia

He gave to Alexander; to Ptolemy he assigned
Syria, Cilicia and Phoenicia. She
In th' habiliments of the goddess Isis
That day appeared, and oft before gave audience,
As 'tis reported, so.

act 3, scene 6, lines 1–19

The crowning iniquity, in Roman judgment, is that Cleopatra's assumption of divinity completes Antony's "treason" in dividing the empire.

Maecenas: Let Rome be thus informed.
Agrippa: Who, queasy with his insolence already,
Will their good thoughts call from him.
Octavius: The people knows it, and have now received
His accusations.
Agrippa: Who does he accuse?
Octavius: Caesar, and that, having in Sicily
Sextus Pompeius spoiled, we had not rated him
His part o'th' isle. Then does he say he lent me
Some shipping, unrestored. Lastly, he frets
That Lepidus of the triumvirate
Should be deposed, and, being, that we detain
All his revenue.
Agrippa: Sir, this should be answered.
Octavius: 'Tis done already, and the messenger gone.
I have told him Lepidus was grown too cruel,
That he his high authority abused
And did deserve his change. For what I have conquered,

CLEOPATRA: I AM FIRE AND AIR

I grant him part; but then in his Armenia,
And other of his conquered kingdoms, I
Demand the like.
Maecenas: He'll never yield to that.
Octavius: Nor must not then be yielded to in this.

act 3, scene 6, lines 20–39

In disdain of Rome, Cleopatra and Antony are crowned empress and emperor of the East. Caesarion, the son Julius Caesar begot upon Cleopatra, rouses Octavius to a particular bitterness. He in fact was not the son of Julius Caesar but the grandnephew adopted by Caesar as his heir. After the death of Cleopatra, Octavius ordered Caesarion to be executed.

Attired as the goddess Isis, Cleopatra moves toward her final epiphany at Actium where Antony prepares for the decisive battle with Octavius. Over the strong objections of Enobarbus, Cleopatra insists she will lead her fleet so as not to be parted from Antony. Both lovers court destruction by overriding Enobarbus and choosing to fight by sea rather than land.

Cleopatra provokes disaster by fleeing the battle with all her ships. The disgrace of Antony is a shock to his most loyal commanders:

Enobarbus: Naught, naught, all naught! I can behold no longer!
Th'*Antoniad*, the Egyptian admiral,
With all their sixty, fly and turn the rudder.
To see't mine eyes are blasted. [*Enter Scarus*]
Scarus: Gods and goddesses!
All the whole synod of them!

45

Enobarbus: What's thy passion?
Scarus: The greater cantle of the world is lost
With very ignorance; we have kissed away
Kingdoms and provinces.
Enobarbus: How appears the fight?
Scarus: On our side, like the tokened pestilence,
Where death is sure. Yon ribaudred nag of Egypt—
Whom leprosy o'ertake!—i'th' midst o'th' fight,
When vantage like a pair of twins appeared
Both as the same, or, rather ours the elder,
The breeze upon her, like a cow in June,
Hoists sails and flies.
Enobarbus: That I beheld.
Mine eyes did sicken at the sight and could not
Endure a further view.
Scarus: She once being loofed,
The noble ruin of her magic, Antony,
Claps on his sea wing and, like a doting mallard,
Leaving the fight in height, flies after her.
I never saw an action of such shame.
Experience, manhood, honor, ne'er before
Did violate so itself.

act 3, scene 10, lines 1–23

We do not know why Cleopatra flees. The enigma is why Antony sails after her, abandoning his men. Scarus, who will remain loyal to Antony, nevertheless eloquently characterizes his commander's shame as "the noble ruin of her magic."

Enobarbus: Alack, alack!

[*Enter Canidius*]

Canidius: Our fortune on the sea is out of breath,
And sinks most lamentably. Had our general
Been what he knew himself, it had gone well.
Oh, he has given example for our flight
Most grossly by his own!
Enobarbus: Ay, are you thereabouts? Why then, good night indeed.
Canidius: Toward Peloponnesus are they fled.
Scarus: 'Tis easy to't, and there I will attend
What further comes.
Canidius: To Caesar will I render
My legions and my horse. Six kings already
Show me the way of yielding.
Enobarbus: I'll yet follow
The wounded chance of Antony, though my reason
Sits in the wind against me.

act 3, scene 10, lines 23–36

The image of the downward wind opens and closes this sequence. Turning her ship's head close to the wind and thus choosing distance, Cleopatra runs away. Antony flees like a water bird, a doting male duck, his nobility collapsing. Like Scarus, Enobarbus realizes he will be tracked and hunted down like a dying wind and yet struggles to remain loyal.

What animates Cleopatra? Is it cowardice? Can it be deliberate treachery? Or is this her vengeance, on whatever level of awareness, for Antony's expedient marriage to Octavia? It may well be all three and more. So complex is her nature that we want to call it divided but we would err. She is so artful that we never can know her motivations. Nor can she.

47

What we can perceive is that Cleopatra and the entire tragi-comedy is profoundly Ovidian, unsurprising since the Roman poet Ovid was a major influence on Shakespeare and many of his contemporaries. Cleopatra is metamorphic to a fault. She flows and ebbs and returns in full vigor. Antony, like Ovid's Hercules, goes from woman to woman until he meets his bright culmination and destruction in Cleopatra.

In Ovid all identity flows and then merges with fresh identities. Cleopatra, unlike Antony, retains her essential being. Like the Nile she inundates and then brings forth a harvest of burgeoning vivaciousness. Metamorphic, she yet overcomes change through histrionic genius. She acts and is, and who can tell what in her is not theatrical?

Antony, bereft of authority and of honor, provokes Cleopatra into one of her histrionic transports:

Eros: Nay, gentle madam, to him, comfort him.

Iras: Do, most dear Queen.

Charmian: Do; why, what else?

Cleopatra: Let me sit down. O Juno!

Antony: No, no, no, no, no.

Eros: See you here, sir?

Antony: O fie, fie, fie!

Charmian: Madam!

Iras: Madam! O, good Empress!

Eros: Sir, sir!

Antony: Yes, my lord, yes. He at Philippi kept
His sword e'en like a dancer, while I struck
The lean and wrinkled Cassius, and 'twas I

That the mad Brutus ended. He alone
Dealt on lieutenantry, and no practice had
In the brave squares of war; yet now—no matter.

act 3, scene 11, lines 25–40

On the verge of fainting, a skill at which she is superb, Cleopatra is led to her lover, who is overwhelmed by self-disgust. Tell-
ingly, his particular bitterness is that he, a great swordsman and
leader in battle, must now yield to Octavius, who fought only
through his underlings and kept his ornamental sword sheathed
like a dancer in performance. His reproach to Cleopatra is searing:
"Oh, whither hast thou led me, Egypt?"

Cleopatra: Ah, stand by.
Eros: The Queen, my lord, the Queen.
Iras: Go to him, madam, speak to him.
He is unqualitied with very shame.
Cleopatra: Well then, sustain me. Oh!
Eros: Most noble sir, arise. The Queen approaches.
Her head's declined, and death will seize her but
Your comfort makes the rescue.
Antony: I have offended reputation,
A most unnoble swerving.
Eros: Sir, the Queen.
Antony: O, whither hast thou led me, Egypt? See
How I convey my shame out of thine eyes
By looking back what I have left behind
'Stroyed in dishonor.
Cleopatra: Oh, my lord, my lord,

Forgive my fearful sails! I little thought
You would have followed.

Antony: Egypt, thou knew'st too well
My heart was to thy rudder tied by th' strings,
And thou shouldst tow me after. O'er my spirit
Thy full supremacy thou knew'st, and that
Thy beck might from the bidding of the gods
Command me.

act 3, scene 11, lines 41–60

Is this still Antony? Can we be moved by this pathetic complaint?

Cleopatra: Oh, my pardon!
Antony: Now I must
To the young man send humble treaties, dodge
And palter in the shifts of lowness, who
With half the bulk o'th' world played as I pleased,
Making and marring fortunes. You did know
How much you were my conqueror, and that
My sword, made weak by my affection, would
Obey it on all cause.
Cleopatra: Pardon, pardon!
Antony: Fall not a tear, I say; one of them rates
All that is won and lost. Give me a kiss.   [*They kiss*]
Even this repays me.—We sent our schoolmaster;
Is 'a come back?—Love, I am full of lead.—
Some wine, within there, and our viands! Fortune knows
We scorn her most when most she offers blows.

act 3, scene 11, lines 60–73

Whether or not she is overcome by chagrin or is playing her part, Cleopatra strikingly is reduced to a plea for pardon. Antony, recovering with a tender dignity, calls for a kiss that equals all he has lost. It is one of a series of sad moments that will mark his descent to darkness.

CHAPTER 8

You Will Be Whipped

We go into the dark and will abide there with only a few ascents to light as Antony commences to lose his flowing hold upon vitality and a flawed nobility:

Antony: Is that his answer?

Ambassador: Ay, my lord.

Antony: The Queen shall then have courtesy, so she

Will yield us up.

Ambassador: He says so.

Antony: Let her know't.—

To the boy Caesar send this grizzled head,

And he will fill thy wishes to the brim

With principalities.

Cleopatra: That head, my lord?

Antony: [*to Ambassador*] To him again. Tell him he wears the

rose

Of youth upon him, from which the world should note

Something particular. His coin, ships, legions,

May be a coward's, whose ministers would prevail

Under the service of a child as soon

As i'th' command of Caesar. I dare him therefore

To lay his gay caparisons apart

And answer me declined, sword against sword,
Ourselves alone. I'll write it. Follow me.

[*Exeunt Antony and Ambassador*]

Enobarbus: [*aside*] Yes, like enough, high-battled Caesar will
Unstate his happiness, and be staged to th' show
Against a sworder! I see men's judgments are
A parcel of their fortunes, and things outward
Do draw the inward quality after them
To suffer all alike. That he should dream,
Knowing all measures, the full Caesar will
Answer his emptiness! Caesar, thou hast subdued
His judgment too.

Servant: A messenger from Caesar.

Cleopatra: What, no more ceremony? See, my women,
Against the blown rose may they stop their nose
That kneeled unto the buds.—Admit him, sir.

Enobarbus: [*aside*] Mine honesty and I begin to square.
The loyalty well held to fools does make
Our faith mere folly; yet he that can endure
To follow with allegiance a fall'n lord
Does conquer him that did his master conquer
And earns a place i'th' story.

act 3, scene 13, lines 13–46

It is a delicate moment when Antony tells Cleopatra that his grizzled head will purchase her freedom to hold sway. What is the nuance of: "That head, my lord?" You can hear tenderness but also a surmise that this is her way to go on living and reigning. Enobarbus ruminates that the decline of fortune draws Antony's inward judgment into absurdity. This faithful soldier struggles with the dilemma of loyalty that becomes folly. For now Enobarbus chooses the moral triumph of allegiance over the abyss of a downward trajectory into darkness.

The dialogue between Cleopatra and Thidias, Octavius Caesar's ambassador, shows the Egyptian queen at her insidious power of dissembling:

Cleopatra: Caesar's will?
Thidias: Hear it apart.
Cleopatra: None but friends. Say boldly.
Thidias: So haply are they friends to Antony.
Enobarbus: He needs as many, sir, as Caesar has,
Or needs not us. If Caesar please, our master
Will leap to be his friend. For us, you know
Whose he is we are, and that is Caesar's.
Thidias: So.
Thus then, thou most renowned: Caesar entreats
Not to consider in what case thou stand'st
Further than he is Caesar.
Cleopatra: Go on: right royal.
Thidias: He knows that you embrace not Antony
As you did love, but as you feared him.
Cleopatra: Oh!
Thidias: The scars upon your honor therefore he
Does pity, as constrainèd blemishes,
Not as deserved.
Cleopatra: He is a god and knows
What is most right. Mine honor was not yielded,
But conquered merely.
Enobarbus: [*aside*] To be sure of that,
I will ask Antony. Sir, sir, thou art so leaky

That we must leave thee to thy sinking, for
Thy dearest quit thee.   [*Exit Enobarbus*]
Thidias: Shall I say to Caesar
What you require of him? For he partly begs
To be desired to give. It much would please him
That of his fortunes you should make a staff
To lean upon; but it would warm his spirits
To hear from me you had left Antony
And put yourself under his shroud,
The universal landlord.
Cleopatra: What's your name?
Thidias: My name is Thidias.
Cleopatra: Most kind messenger,
Say to great Caesar this in deputation:
I kiss his conquering hand. Tell him I am prompt
To lay my crown at's feet, and there to kneel
Tell him from his all-obeying breath I hear
The doom of Egypt.

                              act 3, scene 13, lines 46–78

There is dark irony in the suggestion by Thidias that the Egyptian queen abandon Antony and seek shelter under the shroud of the universal landlord, who is both Octavius and death. By the doom of Egypt she means her destiny yet ironically that is death. In the face of fortune at war with wisdom, the wise survivor will desire whatever fortune will grant and thus the vicissitudes of experience may be tempered by sagacity.

Thidias: 'Tis your noblest course.
Wisdom and fortune combating together,

56

If that the former dare but what it can,
No chance may shake it. Give me grace to lay
My duty on your hand.   [*He kisses her hand*]
Cleopatra: Your Caesar's father oft,
When he hath mused of taking kingdoms in,
Bestowed his lips on that unworthy place,
As it rained kisses.

act 3, scene 13, lines 78–86

Antony and Enobarbus enter to find Cleopatra allowing her hand to be kissed by the enemy emissary. What ensues is a detonation of the dying old lion:

Antony: Favors? By Jove that thunders!
What art thou, fellow?
Thidias: One that but performs
The bidding of the fullest man, and worthiest
To have command obeyed.
Enobarbus: [*aside*]   You will be whipped.
Antony: [*Calling for Servants*]
Approach, there!—Ah, you kite!—Now, gods and devils!
Authority melts from me of late. When I cried 'Ho!',
Like boys unto a muss kings would start forth
And cry 'Your will?'—Have you no ears? I am
Antony yet.
                    [*Enter Servant followed by others*]
Take hence the jack and whip him.
Enobarbus: [*aside*] 'Tis better playing with a lion's whelp
Than with an old one dying.

act 3, scene 13, lines 86–96

It scarcely helps the wretched Thidias that he further provokes
Antony by calling Octavius the fullest man or best and most fortunate
and far more worthy to be of aid. In fullest fury Antony with the one
word "kite" skewers Thidias as a screech owl, a bird of prey, and Cleopatra as a whore. In the obsolete sense, muss was a game in which you
threw down small objects and then scrambled for them. The outcry: "I
am Antony yet" contains grief, desperation, and savagery.

Antony: Moon and stars!
Whip him. Were't twenty of the greatest tributaries
That do acknowledge Caesar, should I find them
So saucy with the hand of she here—what's her name
Since she was Cleopatra? Whip him, fellows,
Till, like a boy you see him cringe his face
And whine aloud for mercy. Take him hence.
Thidias: Mark Antony—
Antony: Tug him away! Being whipped,
Bring him again. This Jack of Caesar's shall
Bear us an errand to him.

act 3, scene 13, lines 96–105

He slashes at the Queen with the caustic "what's her name / Since
she was Cleopatra?" Terrible sadism is caught up in the order to whip
Thidias until he contracts in pain. It is also sadistic rhetoric as Antony
calls Cleopatra a boggler, shifty as a shying horse. The Herculean
hero's misery carries him to the image of his eyes seeled or blinded
by the gods. They laugh at him while he struts to his self-destruction.

Antony: You were half blasted ere I knew you. Ha?
Have I my pillow left unpressed in Rome,

Forborne the getting of a lawful race,
And by a gem of women, to be abused
By one that looks on feeders?
Cleopatra: Good my lord—
Antony: You have been a boggler ever.
But when we in our viciousness grow hard—
O misery on't!—the wise gods seel our eyes,
In our own filth drop our clear judgments, make us
Adore our errors, laugh at's while we strut
To our confusion.
Cleopatra: Oh, is't come to this?
Antony: I found you as a morsel, cold upon
Dead Caesar's trencher; nay, you were a fragment
Of Gnaeus Pompey's, besides what hotter hours,
Unregistered in vulgar fame, you have
Luxuriously picked out. For I am sure,
Though you can guess what temperance should be,
You know not what it is.
Cleopatra: Wherefore is this?
Antony: To let a fellow that will take rewards
And say 'God quit you!' be familiar with
My playfellow, your hand, this kingly seal
And plighter of high hearts! Oh, that I were
Upon the hill of Basan, to outroar
The hornèd herd! For I have savage cause,
And to proclaim it civilly were like
A haltered neck which does the hangman thank
For being yare about him.

act 3, scene 13, lines 106–33

His contempt for the Egyptian queen hardly could go beyond the nastiness of calling her a scrap of meat cold upon Julius Caesar's platter and the leftover of Pompey's gorging. Her bewilderment is uncharacteristic but overwhelming. With his gift for salient anachronism, Shakespeare invokes the great bulls of Bashan.

> Many young bulls have compassed me: mighty bulls of Bashan have closed me about.
>
> They gape upon me with their mouths, *as* a ramping and roaring lion.
>
> Psalm 22:12–13, Geneva Bible

The implication is that Antony sees himself as a horned beast or cuckold. He roars civility away lest he be as one, about to be hanged, who thanks the hangman for being handy and quick. Shakespeare entertained no illusions about Antony. Plutarch, who hated Antony, nevertheless seems accurate enough in his depiction of Roman savagery. The historical Mark Antony was a bloodthirsty butcher. If he differed at all from the cold and calculating Octavius Caesar, it was in passion, hedonistic excess, and the relish he tasted in sadism. Anyone who reads Cicero, as I do frequently, is horrified that the magnificent orator, philosopher, and prose stylist was slaughtered by Antony's soldiers in revenge for the speeches in which he had excoriated their leader. Mark Antony rejoiced in displaying the severed head and hands of Cicero in the Roman Forum.

You can of course observe that Shakespeare's Antony is after all his own creation. Capacious as always, Shakespeare shows us more than enough to alienate us from both Antony and Cleopatra, but that is not his way. They do not move us either to empathy or to sympathy. And yet their imaginative largeness wounds our consciousness. Falstaff beguiles me to the heart of loss. I feel within me the anguish of his rejection by Hal. And how can one not lament the diminishment of joy and vitality when we move from the two parts of *Henry IV* to the brilliant yet hollow *Henry V*?

Shakespeare at his strongest still seems beyond our apprehension. I rarely can find words precise enough to surmise his stance in regard to his major protagonists. I come to assume he shares the appreciation of their high style of speech and existence he induces in us. They live and move and have their being in realms touching the limits of the human. Antony is a Bacchus or Dionysus as well as a Hercules. The Egyptian Dionysus was Osiris and Antony dies the death of Hercules scattered into the *sparagmos* of Dionysus-Osiris. Isis was the Egyptian Aphrodite or Venus, a role made flesh in Cleopatra. She gathers the limbs of Osiris for his rebirth. Though Cleopatra finally has a vision of a reunion with Antony in the Elysian Fields as she dies, are we convinced?

For a lifetime I have pondered Shakespeare's perspectivism and wonder if ever I can comprehend it. His incredible sweep and agile otherseeing (to call it that) always return me to the realization I cannot get outside of him. All of us repose within his benign containment. The miracle of his Rosalind in *As You Like It* is that her clarity and normative temperament happily prevent us from any ironic perspective we might seek to gain power over her. She is herself the compass of her world.

It is palpable that Shakespeare affords us many ironic perspectives in regard to Cleopatra and Antony. If we can see what they cannot, that privilege does not diminish their shared appreciation of each other. Is that mutual esteem a sublime form of love or is it two opulent grandees seeking their reflections in the eyes of the other?

Except for Shakespeare and Plato, the poet who best knew the essence of love was Shelley:

The great secret of morals is Love; or a going out of our own nature, and an identification of ourselves with the beautiful which exists in thought, action, or person, not our own.

"On Love"

By that High Romantic test we would have to say that Cleopatra loves Cleopatra and Antony loves Antony. But who can say of anyone that they are not in love? Cleopatra and Antony betray each other, return, and always Cleopatra is tempted to betray again. She is a queen whose throne is in jeopardy. Reality abandons him. From grandeur he is reduced to grandiosity.

Yet they never lose their supreme interest for us. Shakespeare's endless art heaps wonder upon wonder. Personality triumphs in Falstaff and Cleopatra. If character is fate, then in a harsh sense there can be no accidents. Personalities suffer accidents; characters endure fate.

The test for a strong personality is to surmount accidents. Antony falls away from personality and meets the fate inherent in his character. Falstaff is broken, but only after his marvelous personality dissipates. Cleopatra, perhaps the strongest of all Shakespeare's personalities, dies upward into a sublime beyond as Hamlet did.

Yet he rests in silence. Cleopatra's apotheosis achieves divinity. The water and soil of the Nile and Egypt are purged. She becomes fire and air.

Only Shakespeare could convince us that she does not vanish into Isis the mystery. She is Cleopatra still. That rare spirit of amorous dalliance is also the difference that enduring personality enhances between the Egyptian queen and her lost Antony. She knows not loss nor the death of illusion. For her, desire can never fail.

The contrast with Antony hardly could be greater. His courage transmutes into wounded desperation. One of his low points is the message he tells the wretched Thidias to deliver to Octavius:

> **Antony:**   Get thee back to Caesar.
> Tell him thy entertainment. Look thou say
> He makes me angry with him; for he seems
> Proud and disdainful, harping on what I am,
> Not what he knew I was. He makes me angry,
> And at this time most easy 'tis to do't,
> When my good stars, that were my former guides,
> Have empty left their orbs and shot their fires
> Into th'abysm of hell. If he mislike
> My speech and what is done, tell him he has
> Hipparchus, my enfranchèd bondman, whom
> He may at pleasure whip, or hang, or torture,
> As he shall like, to quit me. Urge it thou.
> Hence with thy stripes, begone!
> **Cleopatra:**   Have you done yet?
> **Antony:** Alack, our terrene moon is now eclipsed,
> And it portends alone the fall of Antony.

Cleopatra: I must stay his time.

Antony: To flatter Caesar, would you mingle eyes

With one that ties his points?

Cleopatra: Not know me yet?

Antony: Coldhearted toward me?

act 3, scene 13, lines 142–61

It is sorrowful to call Antony ignoble, but what else can we say when he suggests that Octavian requite the suffering of Thidias by whipping, hanging, torturing, or what you will, one Hipparchus, Antony's freedman who was going over to the enemy. The brutality mixes with the pitiful lament that his stars have shot their fires into the abyss. Cleopatra, patiently awaiting the ebbing of his fury, listens to his double plaint that the eclipsed moon foretells demise and that Isis, goddess of the moon, as Cleopatra has withdrawn her love for him.

Her protestations satisfy him and enhance his lust for the final battle:

Antony: I will be treble-sinewed, hearted, breathed,

And fight maliciously. For when mine hours

Were nice and lucky, men did ransom lives

Of me for jests; but now, I'll set my teeth

And send to darkness all that stop me. Come,

Let's have one other gaudy night. Call to me

All my sad captains. Fill our bowls once more;

Let's mock the midnight bell.

Cleopatra: It is my birthday.

I had thought t'have held it poor, but since my lord

Is Antony again, I will be Cleopatra.

Antony: We will yet do well.

Cleopatra: [*to Charmian and attendants*] Call all his noble
captains to my lord.

Antony: Do so. We'll speak to them, and tonight I'll force
The wine peep through their scars. Come on, my queen,
There's sap in't yet. The next time I do fight
I'll make Death love me, for I will contend
Even with his pestilent scythe.

act 3, scene 13, lines 181–97

His call for another festive night is tempered by the beautiful:
"All my sad captains." It is Cleopatra's birthday and the sap of life
rises again in Antony. We hear in Enobarbus the accents of farewell:

Now he'll outstare the lightning. To be furious
Is to be frighted out of fear, and in that mood
The dove will peck the estridge; and I see still
A diminution in our captain's brain
Restores his heart. When valor preys on reason,
It eats the sword it fights with. I will seek
Some way to leave him.

act 3, scene 13, lines 198–204

Ironic old warrior as he is, Enobarbus rightly knows that reason-
able courage in battle was the foundation of Antony's past glory.
The fresh heart of the great captain is purchased at the cost of a
diminishment in mind. Most loyal of Antony's followers, he now
despairs and resolves on desertion. The dying music of Antony's
glory reverberates in this abandonment.

CHAPTER 9

The God Hercules Withdraws

Approaching his end, Antony moves us through his pathos, if perhaps a touch too self-pitying:

Antony: Well, my good fellows, wait on me tonight;
Scant not my cups, and make as much of me
As when mine empire was your fellow too,
And suffered my command.
Cleopatra: [*aside to Enobarbus*] What does he mean?
Enobarbus: [*aside to Cleopatra*]
To make his followers weep.
Antony: Tend me tonight;
May be it is the period of your duty.
Haply you shall not see me more, or if,
A mangled shadow. Perchance tomorrow
You'll serve another master. I look on you
As one that takes his leave. Mine honest friends,
I turn you not away, but, like a master
Married to your good service, stay till death.
Tend me tonight two hours, I ask no more,
And the gods yield you for't!

Enobarbus: What mean you, sir,
To give them this discomfort? Look, they weep,
And I, an ass, am onion-eyed. For shame,
Transform us not to women.
Antony: Ho, ho, ho!
Now the witch take me if I meant it thus!
Grace grow where those drops fall! My hearty friends,
You take me in too dolorous a sense,
For I spake to you for your comfort, did desire you
To burn this night with torches. Know, my hearts,
I hope well of tomorrow, and will lead you
Where rather I'll expect victorious life
Than death and honor. Let's to supper, come,
And drown consideration.

act 4, scene 2, lines 21–46

His sad captains weep; even Enobarbus joins in but then remonstrates with Antony. Something crucial is departing from the flawed hero. Partly following Plutarch, Shakespeare reveals the supernatural abandonment of Antony by his daemon or guiding genius:

First Soldier: Brother, good night. Tomorrow is the day.
Second Soldier: It will determine one way. Fare you well.
Heard you of nothing strange about the streets?
First Soldier: Nothing. What news?
Second Soldier: Belike 'tis but a rumor. Good night to you.
First Soldier: Well, sir, good night. [*They meet other Soldiers*]
Second Soldier: Soldiers, have careful watch.
Third Soldier: And you. Good night, good night.

Second Soldier: Here we. And if tomorrow
Our navy thrive, I have an absolute hope
Our landmen will stand up.

First Soldier: 'Tis a brave army, and full of purpose.

[*Music of the hautboys as under the stage*]

Second Soldier: Peace! What noise?

First Soldier: List, list!

Second Soldier: Hark!

First Soldier: Music i'th'air.

Third Soldier: Under the earth.

Fourth Soldier: It signs well, does it not?

Third Soldier: No.

First Soldier: Peace, I say! What should this mean?

Second Soldier: 'Tis the god Hercules, whom Antony loved
Now leaves him.

First Soldier: Walk; let's see if other watchmen
Do hear what we do.   [*They advance toward their fellow
     watchmen*]

Second Soldier: How now, masters?

All: How now? How now? Do you hear this?

First Soldier: Ay. Is't not strange?

Third Soldier: Do you hear, masters? Do you hear?

First Soldier: Follow the noise so far as we have quarter;
Let's see how it will give off.

All: Content. 'Tis strange.

act 4, scene 3, lines 1–30

In Plutarch the departing daemon is Dionysus or Bacchus. Shakespeare chooses Hercules because Antony is the very archetype of the Herculean hero. Indeed he claimed descent from Hercules and prided himself that he looked like his mythological ancestor. Always subtle, Shakespeare implies that Antony became Dionysus or Osiris in his scattering but was Herculean at his apex.

The withdrawal of the god, be he Bacchus or Hercules, initiates from the opening lines of *Antony and Cleopatra* and concludes with his piteous death:

> Now my spirit is going;
> I can no more.
>
> act 4, scene 15, lines 60–61

There is an uncanny magic in Shakespeare's music below the stage and in the air. I hear a faint echo of the ghost of Hamlet's father in the early scenes of that most enigmatic of all dramas. Yet this in *Antony and Cleopatra* is somehow stranger:

> 'Tis the god Hercules, whom Antony loved
> Now leaves him.

The plangency of this abandonment is enhanced if you substitute "the goddess Isis" for "the god Hercules." We are not told that Hercules loved Antony or that Isis the mystery was in love with him. There is a panic in Antony throughout this vast play that Cleopatra might fall out of love with him. Despite his bravura, something in him knows that without her vitality he will go on ebbing.

Does she ever fall out of love with him? Wavering is her metamorphic mode. An absolute realist, she knows before he does that Antony wanes. All of Shakespeare's strongest women are survivalists and Cleopatra is preeminent among them. We need not doubt her passion for Antony and yet she would sell him out for the right price. When Antony calls her "the armorer of my heart" and his next words are "false, false," he thinks he means that Cleopatra is adjusting his armor wrongly. Scarcely ever can Antony overhear himself. Shakespeare's art is in the irony that Antony's heart will be played false.

Marching toward the last battle with Octavius, Antony receives the news that Enobarbus has deserted him, leaving his treasure as a gesture to the gods that he goes half-unwillingly. Antony's nobility returns in his own gracious gesture:

Go, Eros, send his treasure after. Do it.
Detain no jot, I charge thee. Write to him—
I will subscribe—gentle adieus and greetings.
Say that I wish he never find more cause
To change a master. Oh, my fortunes have
Corrupted honest men! Dispatch.—Enobarbus!

act 4, scene 5, lines 12–17

There is authentic anguish and chagrin in that cry: "Enobarbus!" Shakespeare, in a brilliant juxtaposition, answers that cry with Octavius Caesar, who will be the Emperor Augustus, proclaiming "the time of universal peace is near." This will be the Roman Peace purchased by brutality at home and abroad.

Enobarbus proceeds to his sorrowful extinction:

I have done ill,
Of which I do accuse myself so sorely
That I will joy no more.

act 4, scene 6, lines 18–20

The heavy heart of Enobarbus cannot sustain Antony's final generosity:

Soldier: Enobarbus, Antony
Hath after thee sent all thy treasure, with
His bounty overplus. The messenger
Came on my guard, and at thy tent is now
Unloading of his mules.
Enobarbus: I give it you.
Soldier: Mock not, Enobarbus.
I tell you true. Best you safed the bringer
Out of the host. I must attend mine office,
Or would have done't myself. Your emperor
Continues still a Jove. [*Exit*]
Enobarbus: I am alone the villain of the earth,
And feel I am so most. O Antony,
Thou mine of bounty, how wouldst thou have paid
My better service, when my turpitude
Thou dost so crown with gold! This blows my heart.
If swift thought break it not, a swifter mean
Shall outstrike thought, but thought will do't, I feel.
I fight against thee? No, I will go seek
Some ditch wherein to die. The foul'st best fits
My latter part of life.

act 4, scene 6, lines 20–40

Throughout the play we have enjoyed Enobarbus for his wit, realism, and gusto. Shakespeare must have known how sadly we are moved by the irony that Antony's generosity drives Enobarbus to suicide. That sorrow is enhanced by his portrayal of the last moments of Enobarbus:

Sentry: If we be not relieved within this hour,
We must return to th' court of guard. The night
Is shiny, and they say we shall embattle
By th' second hour i' th' morn.
First Watch: This last day was a shrewd one to 's.
Enobarbus: O bear me witness, night—
Second Watch: What man is this?
First Watch: Stand close, and list him.   [*They stand aside*]
Enobarbus: Be witness to me, O thou blessèd moon,
When men revolted shall upon record
Bear hateful memory: poor Enobarbus did
Before thy face repent.
Sentry: Enobarbus?
Second Watch: Peace! Hark further.
Enobarbus: O sovereign mistress of true melancholy,
The poisonous damp of night disponge upon me,
That life, a very rebel to my will,
May hang no longer on me. Throw my heart
Against the flint and hardness of my fault,
Which, being dried with grief, will break to powder
And finish all foul thoughts. O Antony,
Nobler than my revolt is infamous,
Forgive me in thine own particular,
But let the world rank me in register
A master-leaver and a fugitive.
O Antony! O Antony!   [*He dies*]

First Watch: Let's speak to him.

Sentry: Let's hear him, for the things he speaks
May concern Caesar.

Second Watch: Let's do so. But he sleeps.

Sentry: Swoons rather, for so bad a prayer as his
Was never yet for sleep.

First Watch: Go we to him.

Second Watch: Awake sir, awake. Speak to us.

First Watch: Hear you, sir?

Sentry: The hand of death hath raught him.   [*Drums afar off*]
Hark, the drums demurely wake the sleepers.
Let us bear him to th' court of guard;
He is of note. Our hour is fully out.

Second Watch: Come on, then. He may recover yet.

act 4, scene 9, lines 1–38

Enobarbus with his last breath cries out: "O Antony! O
Antony!" Just before the end he achieves a curious eloquence when
he addresses the moon as: "O sovereign mistress of true melancholy." Whether or not that melancholy is the madness attributed
to the moon's influence, or his own anguish, it stands for the agony
of lost honor that destroys Enobarbus.

CHAPTER 10

This Foul Egyptian Hath Betrayed Me

Antony goes into the battle of Actium with forced confidence:

> I would they'd fight i'th' fire or i'th' air;
> We'd fight there too.
>
> act 4, scene 10, lines 3–4

Disaster is almost immediate:

Scarus: Swallows have built
In Cleopatra's sails their nests. The augurers
Say they know not, they cannot tell, look grimly,
And dare not speak their knowledge. Antony
Is valiant, and dejected, and by starts,
His fretted fortunes give him hope and fear
Of what he has and has not.   [*Enter Antony*]
Antony: All is lost!
This foul Egyptian hath betrayèd me.
My fleet hath yielded to the foe, and yonder
They cast their caps up and carouse together
Like friends long lost. Triple-turned whore! 'Tis thou

Hast sold me to this novice, and my heart
Makes only wars on thee. Bid them all fly;
For when I am revenged upon my charm,
I have done all. Bid them all fly. Be gone!   [*Exit Scarus*]
O sun, thy uprise shall I see no more.
Fortune and Antony part here; even here
Do we shake hands. All come to this? The hearts
That spanieled me at heels, to whom I gave
Their wishes, do discandy, melt their sweets
On blossoming Caesar; and this pine is barked
That overtopped them all. Betrayed I am.
O this false soul of Egypt! This grave charm,
Whose eye becked forth my wars and called them home,
Whose bosom was my crownet, my chief end,
Like a right gipsy hath at fast and loose
Beguiled me to the very heart of loss.
[*Calling*] What, Eros, Eros!

                                        act 4, scene 12, 3–30

Antony's vexed fortunes have him in wild alternation between vain hope and the foreboding of loss. When his fleet, with many Egyptian ships, goes over to Octavius he sensibly concludes that Cleopatra has sold him out. The immensely bitter: "Triple-turned whore" hits at the sequence of Julius Caesar, Pompey, and Antony himself. He endures now only to avenge himself on her evil magic and invokes the sunrise he will not live to see.

   The hearts
That spanieled me at heels, to whom I gave
Their wishes, do discandy, melt their sweets

On blossoming Caesar; and this pine is barked
That overtopped them all.

There is a gracious turn in parting from fortune on good
terms and then a falling into self-pity as he chides the false-
hearted former followers whom he enriched. There is some
question as to the word "spannell'd." The Folio text reads "pan-
nelled," which was amended to "spanieled." In Shakespeare's day
"pannell" meant a whore, and that fits the context better, since it
applies both to the followers abandoning Antony and to Cleopatra. They dissolve and melt as tributaries to the blossoming
Octavius and he, solitary pine tree that stood above them all,
is now destroyed by the stripping away of his bark and thus his
life.

Betrayed by the fatal charm of Cleopatra the sorceress, who in
their sexual union had been the culmination of his career and his
destiny, and who had enlisted him in a cheating game, he utters a
line so memorable that Shakespeare could not surpass it:

Beguiled me to the very heart of loss.

Cleopatra enters to be waved away as a false enchantress. What
are we to make of her:

Why is my lord enraged against his love?
act 4, scene 12, line 31

It is difficult to believe she has not connived at the desertion of their combined fleet. Shakespeare will not tell us if she
has intrigued with Octavius to save herself. Certainly her politic

nature suggests such a plot. Why should a goddess and great ruler not seek what is best for Egypt herself?

It has been marvelous that a single play, however prodigious, should have been able for so long to contain two gigantic charismatic personalities. Antony dies near the end of Act 4. From the thirty or so final lines until Act 5, Cleopatra is alone at the center of desolation and loss. In the more than four hundred lines of the final act we see, hear, and are concerned with Cleopatra alone. The great presence of Antony becomes a sepulchral absence.

Shakespeare in *Macbeth* allows Lady Macbeth to speak for the last time in the initial scene of Act V. Four scenes later we hear her women cry out at her death, presumably by suicide. The final act belongs to Macbeth alone. It cannot be said that Lady Macbeth haunts the sequence of heightening equivocations that take us to Macduff's triumphant outcry: "The time is free!"

The imminent departure of Antony compels a reflection upon Shakespeare's extraordinary originality in teaching us that personality fuses presence and the charismatic secularization of the blessing, or being favored by God. What is presence? We tend to use it as charisma, an aura, or the force of what we call personality. Ultimately this has to be traced to the presence of God, whether among all humans, or in each human being, or in nature.

Antony and Cleopatra catches the moment when Rome overcame the Eastern world and ended an era that began with the conquests of Alexander the Great. Alexandria and its eclectic culture yielded to the monolithic Roman Empire. Antony as he goes down is the last representative of a heroic age in which men and gods mingled yet contested one another. Julius Caesar, Antony's leader and hero, is portrayed by Shakespeare in *The Tragedy of Julius Caesar* as already declining before he is assassinated. Octavius Caesar, the Emperor Augustus, is colorless and has the presence of a consummate bureaucrat. It is not possible either to dislike him or to admire his ruthlessness, since he has no personality. The shattering of Mark Antony and subsequent apotheosis by suicide of Cleopatra sorrows us, not for them, but for the disappearance of overwhelming presences.

The presence of the wounded lion Antony is painful to behold and hear as he roars his rage:

> Vanish, or I shall give thee thy deserving
> And blemish Caesar's triumph. Let him take thee
> And hoist thee up to the shouting plebeians!
> Follow his chariot, like the greatest spot
> Of all thy sex; most monster-like be shown
> For poor'st diminutives, for dolts, and let
> Patient Octavia plough thy visage up
> With her prepared nails!　　　[*Exit Cleopatra*]
> 'Tis well thou'rt gone,
> If it be well to live; but better 'twere
> Thou fell'st into my fury, for one death
> Might have prevented many.—Eros, ho!—
> The shirt of Nessus is upon me. Teach me,
> Alcides, thou mine ancestor, thy rage.
> Let me lodge Lichas on the horns o'th' moon,
> And with those hands, that grasped the heaviest club,
> Subdue my worthiest self. The witch shall die.
> To the young Roman boy she hath sold me, and I fall
> Under this plot. She dies for't.—Eros, ho!
>
> 　　　　　　act 4, scene 12, lines 32–49

The invective of terming Cleopatra the greatest disgrace of her gender yields, with her exit, to an astonishing epiphany in which Antony identifies totally with his ancestor Alcides or Hercules who died in agony, poisoned by the bloody shirt of the centaur Nessus, and tossing his hapless page Lichas into the air. Resolving to murder Cleopatra, Antony calls out for his freedman Eros.

Cleopatra in her flight to what will be her tomb compares the fury of Antony to that of Ajax Telamon, who after the fall of Troy erupted into insanity and suicide when the shield and armor of Achilles was not awarded to him. She invokes also the wild Thessalian boar whom Artemis or Diana sent out to destroy the fields of Calydon until it was slaughtered by Meleager. One admires Cleopatra's command of language when she compares the embossed beast to Antony, who also rages in his hopeless exhaustion.

Charmian devises the deception of playing dead and Cleopatra, supreme actress, elaborates it:

Charmian: To th' monument!
There lock yourself and send him word you are dead.
The soul and body rive not more in parting
Than greatness going off.
Cleopatra: To th' monument!
Mardian, go tell him I have slain myself.
Say that the last I spoke was 'Antony,'
And word it, prithee, piteously. Hence, Mardian,
And bring me how he takes my death. To th' monument!

act 4, scene 13, lines 3–10

Whatever her culpability, Cleopatra sensibly does not wish to be butchered by her ferocious lover. When next we see him with Eros, his fury has abated. Replacing it is a speculative mood strangely reminiscent of Hamlet:

> **Hamlet:** Do you see yonder cloud that's almost in shape of a
>   camel?
> **Polonius:** By th' mass and 'tis like a camel indeed.
> **Hamlet:** Methinks it is like a weasel.
> **Polonius:** It is backed like a weasel.
> **Hamlet:** Or like a whale?
> **Polonius:** Very like a whale.
>
> act 3, scene 2, lines 368–73

Hamlet sports with poor Polonius in an exchange that delighted Herman Melville. The volatile Prince of Denmark jests as we would expect him to do. Antony moves and astonishes us by a mood unexpected yet revelatory of his impending metamorphosis:

> **Antony:** Eros, thou yet behold'st me?
> **Eros:**   Ay, noble lord.
> **Antony:** Sometime we see a cloud that's dragonish,
> A vapor sometime like a bear or lion,
> A towered citadel, a pendent rock,
> A forkèd mountain, or blue promontory
> With trees upon't that nod unto the world
> And mock our eyes with air. Thou hast seen these signs;
> They are black vesper's pageants.
> **Eros:**   Ay, my lord.
> **Antony:** That which is now a horse, even with a thought
> The rack dislimns and makes it indistinct
> As water is in water.

Eros: It does, my lord.

Antony: My good knave Eros, now thy captain is
Even such a body. Here I am Antony,
Yet cannot hold this visible shape, my knave.
I made these wars for Egypt, and the Queen,
Whose heart I thought I had, for she had mine—
Which whilst it was mine had annexed unto't
A million more, now lost—she, Eros, has
Packed cards with Caesar and false-played my glory
Unto an enemy's triumph.
Nay, weep not, gentle Eros. There is left us
Ourselves to end ourselves.

                    act 4, scene 14, lines 1–22

There is an immense richness in Antony's: "Eros, thou yet behold'st me?" The faithful Eros is puzzled and acquiescent rather in the manner of Horatio. Staring up at the clouds, hardly a usual pastime, Antony is aware of a lost sense of being and finds in particular clouds emblems of his dissolution. He reads them in the fading glory of sunset presaging the advent of night. The sun has set upon him and the night beckons. As the cloud mass changes shape it dissolves as water falling into water.

Affectionately addressing Eros as a beloved lad, Antony tries to express his baffled awareness of his cloudlike condition, drifting from form to form. The grim image of Cleopatra and Octavius having stacked the deck and thus played crookedly afflicts this Herculean hero into the unexpected quibble of losing to a trump card that becomes a Roman triumph.

When the eunuch Mardian, sent by Cleopatra with the false

news of her death, delivers his message, we hear in Antony an unprecedented grace of farewell:

Antony: Oh, thy vile lady!
She has robbed me of my sword.
Mardian: No, Antony,
My mistress loved thee, and her fortunes mingled
With thine entirely.
Antony: Hence, saucy eunuch, peace!
She hath betrayed me and shall die the death.
Mardian: Death of one person can be paid but once,
And that she has discharged. What thou wouldst do
Is done unto thy hand. The last she spake
Was, 'Antony, most noble Antony!'
Then in the midst a tearing groan did break
The name of Antony; it was divided
Between her heart and lips. She rendered life
Thy name so buried in her.
Antony: Dead, then?
Mardian: Dead.
Antony: Unarm, Eros. The long day's task is done,
And we must sleep. [*to Mardian*] That thou depart'st hence
    safe
Does pay thy labor richly; go. [*Exit Mardian*]
           Off, pluck off! [*Eros unarms him*]
The sevenfold shield of Ajax cannot keep
The battery from my heart. Oh, cleave, my sides!
Heart, once be stronger than thy continent;
Crack thy frail case! Apace, Eros, apace.

No more a soldier. Bruisèd pieces, go;
You have been nobly borne.—From me awhile.   [*Exit Eros*]
I will o'ertake thee, Cleopatra, and
Weep for my pardon. So it must be, for now
All length is torture; since the torch is out,
Lie down and stray no farther. Now all labor
Mars what it does; yea, very force entangles
Itself with strength. Seal then, and all is done.
Eros!—I come, my queen.—Eros!—Stay for me.
Where souls do couch on flowers we'll hand in hand
And with our sprightly port make the ghosts gaze.
Dido and her Aeneas shall want troops,
And all the haunt be ours. Come, Eros, Eros!

act 4, scene 14, lines 22–54

Antony and Cleopatra is replete with felicities yet there is a sonority unique and vibrant in:

Antony: Dead, then?
Mardian: Dead.
Antony: Unarm, Eros. The long day's task is done,
And we must sleep.

Shakespeare plays beautifully on the name of Eros. The devoted freedman is instructed to remove Antony's armor and Eros, the Greek god of love known as Cupid to the Romans, informs the dying fall of: "The long day's task is done / And we must sleep." The slumber of death is only part of this resonance. Antony's warlike career dies with the supposedly dead Cleopatra.

When Aeneas went down to Hades, he attempted to greet

Dido, whom he had forsaken, but she turned away in scorn. It is wistful of Antony to believe they were reunited in the Underworld but that is his hope for Cleopatra and himself.

Eros enters and Antony proceeds to what will be his bungled suicide:

Eros: What would my lord?

Antony: Since Cleopatra died
I have lived in such dishonor that the gods
Detest my baseness. I, that with my sword
Quartered the world, and o'er green Neptune's back
With ships made cities, condemn myself to lack
The courage of a woman—less noble mind
Than she which, by her death, our Caesar tells
'I am conqueror of myself.' Thou art sworn, Eros,
That when the exigent should come which now
Is come indeed, when I should see behind me
The inevitable prosecution of
Disgrace and horror, that on my command
Thou then wouldst kill me. Do't. The time is come.
Thou strik'st not me, 'tis Caesar thou defeat'st.
Put color in thy cheek.

Eros: The gods withhold me!
Shall I do that which all the Parthian darts,
Though enemy, lost aim and could not?

Antony: Eros,
Wouldst thou be windowed in great Rome and see
Thy master thus with pleached arms, bending down
His corrigible neck, his face subdued
To penetrative shame, whilst the wheeled seat

85

Of fortunate Caesar, drawn before him, branded
His baseness that ensued?

Eros: I would not see't.

Antony: Come, then, for with a wound I must be cured.
Draw that thy honest sword which thou hast worn
Most useful for thy country.

Eros: Oh, sir, pardon me!

Antony: When I did make thee free, swor'st thou not then
To do this when I bade thee? Do it at once,
Or thy precedent services are all
But accidents unpurposed. Draw, and come.

Eros: Turn from me then that noble countenance
Wherein the worship of the whole world lies.

Antony: Lo thee! *[He turns away]*

Eros: My sword is drawn.

Antony: Then let it do at once
The thing why thou hast drawn it.

Eros: My dear master,
My captain and my emperor, let me say,
Before I strike this bloody stroke, farewell.

Antony: 'Tis said, man, and farewell.

Eros: Farewell, great chief. Shall I strike now?

Antony: Now, Eros.

Eros: *[kills himself]* Why, there then! Thus I do escape the sorrow
Of Antony's death.

Antony: Thrice nobler than myself!
Thou teachest me, O valiant Eros, what
I should and thou couldst not! My queen and Eros
Have by their brave instruction got upon me
A nobleness in record. But I will be

86

A bridegroom in my death and run into't
As to a lover's bed. Come, then! And, Eros,
Thy master dies thy scholar. To do thus
I learned of thee.   [*Falls on his sword*]
                    How, not dead? Not dead?
The guard, ho! Oh, dispatch me!

                              act 4, scene 14, lines 55–104

Shakespeare permits himself the irony of Antony commending the still very much alive Cleopatra as defiant of Octavius: "'I am conqueror of myself.'" There is a cold splendor in Antony's nightmare vision of following the triumphal chariot of Octavius Caesar, bound and disgraced. Whether we are moved by this foreboding, the devotion of Eros touches us.

Antony, always aware of his place in history, praises Eros and the deceiving Cleopatra for making him tardy, and then achieves eloquence in:

But I will be
A bridegroom in my death and run into't
As to a lover's bed.

Two years before, in *Measure for Measure*, Shakespeare gave Claudio, condemned to death, an even more spirited declaration:

If I must die,
I will encounter darkness as a bride,
And hug it in mine arms.

                              act 3, scene 1, lines 82–84

A few lines later, Claudio falls away from this to the nadir of urging his sister to prostitute herself, so as to save his life. Antony is nobler but botches his suicide, thus continuing a loss of poise that is the undersong of the entire play.

From now until his death we see Antony at his best, paradoxically achieving a new grandeur:

First Guard: What's the noise?

Antony: I have done my work ill, friends.

Oh, make an end of what I have begun!

Second Guard: The star is fallen.

First Guard: And time is at his period.

All the Guard: Alas, and woe!

Antony: Let him that loves me strike me dead.

First Guard: Not I.

Second Guard: Nor I.

Third Guard: Nor anyone.   [*Exeunt all the Guard but Dercetas*]

Dercetas: Thy death and fortunes bid thy followers fly.

This sword but shown to Caesar with this tidings,

Shall enter me with him.   [*He takes up Antony's sword*]

[*Enter Diomedes*]

Diomedes: Where's Antony?

Dercetas: There, Diomed, there.

Diomedes: Lives he? Wilt thou not answer, man?   [*Exit

Dercetas*]

Antony: Art thou there, Diomed? Draw thy sword, and give

me

Sufficing strokes for death.

Diomedes: Most absolute lord,

My mistress Cleopatra sent me to thee.

Antony: When did she send thee?

Diomedes: Now, my lord.

Antony: Where is she?

Diomedes: Locked in her monument. She had a prophesying fear

Of what hath come to pass. For when she saw—

Which never shall be found—you did suspect

She had disposed with Caesar, and that your rage

Would not be purged, she sent you word she was dead;

But, fearing since how it might work, hath sent

Me to proclaim the truth, and I am come,

I dread, too late.

Antony: Too late, good Diomed. Call my guard, I prithee.

Diomedes: What ho, the Emperor's guard! The guard, what ho!

Come, your lord calls.   [*Enter four or five of the Guard of Antony*]

Antony: Bear me, good friends, where Cleopatra bides.

'Tis the last service that I shall command you.

First Guard: Woe, woe are we, sir! You may not live to wear

All your true followers out.

All the Guard: Most heavy day!

Antony: Nay, good my fellows, do not please sharp fate

To grace it with your sorrows. Bid that welcome

Which comes to punish us, and we punish it,

Seeming to bear it lightly. Take me up.

I have led you oft; carry me now, good friends,

And have my thanks for all.   [*Exeunt, bearing Antony and Eros*]

                    act 4, scene 14, lines 105–45

The rich music returns in:

Second Guard: The star is fallen.
First Guard: And time is at his period.
All: Alas, and woe!

We near the end of an age and Shakespeare allows us to overhear it. Antony is again impressive when he accepts Cleopatra's sham that she died and asks only to see her for a last time. His true spirit breathes and is enhanced by his stoic acceptance:

>   do not please sharp fate
> To grace it with your sorrows. Bid that welcome
> Which comes to punish us, and we punish it,
> Seeming to bear it lightly.

CHAPTER 11

I Am Dying, Egypt, Dying

As Antony dies, Cleopatra sustains herself with high histrionic artistry. Only at the moment of his passing does she cease performing and actually faints, no longer simulating a loss of consciousness. Shakespeare intricately counterpoints this final tryst of the great lovers, playing Antony's agonized concern for her against Cleopatra's intense concern for herself alone:

> **Cleopatra:** Oh, Charmian, I will never go from hence.
> **Charmian:** Be comforted, dear madam.
> **Cleopatra:**   No, I will not.
> All strange and terrible events are welcome,
> But comforts we despise. Our size of sorrow,
> Proportioned to our cause, must be as great
> As that which makes it.   [*Enter Diomedes (below)*]
> How now? Is he dead?
> **Diomedes:** His death's upon him, but not dead.
> Look out o'th'other side your monument;
> His guard have brought him thither.
>   [*Enter (below) Antony, borne by the Guard*]
> **Cleopatra:**   O sun,
> Burn the great sphere thou mov'st in; darkling stand

The varying shore o'th' world! O Antony,
Antony, Antony! Help, Charmian, help, Iras, help!
Help, friends below! Let's draw him hither.
Antony: Peace!
Not Caesar's valor hath o'erthrown Antony,
But Antony's hath triumphed on itself.
Cleopatra: So it should be, that none but Antony
Should conquer Antony; but woe 'tis so!
Antony: I am dying, Egypt, dying. Only
I here importune death awhile, until
Of many thousand kisses the poor last
I lay up thy lips.
Cleopatra: I dare not, dear—
Dear my lord, pardon—I dare not,
Lest I be taken. Not th'imperious show
Of the full-fortuned Caesar ever shall
Be brooched with me. If knife, drugs, serpents, have
Edge, sting, or operation, I am safe.
Your wife Octavia, with her modest eyes
And still conclusion, shall acquire no honor
Demuring upon me. But come, come, Antony—
Help me, my women—we must draw thee up.
Assist, good friends.
Antony: O, quick, or I am gone.

                                                   act 4, scene 15, 1–32

It is difficult to describe the tone Shakespeare grants Cleopatra in this supreme moment of her bereavement. Initially we hear an actress of actresses rehearsing her range of sorrowing:

All strange and terrible events are welcome,
But comforts we despise. Our size of sorrow,
Proportioned to our cause, must be as great
As that which makes it.

It seems curious that Cleopatra is more interested in preparing herself for a great scene than in her supposed suffering. When Antony is carried in, she achieves a self-conscious grandeur in her negative invocation to the sun:

O sun,
Burn the great sphere thou mov'st in; darkling stand
The varying shore o'th' world!

Claudius Ptolemy was a Greco-Egyptian astronomer of the second century of the Common Era who lived in Roman Alexandria and wrote in Koine Greek. In his scheme, the sun rotated around the Earth in a concentric sphere, joined by the planets and the stars. Cleopatra's apocalyptic injunction calls for the sun to incinerate the sphere and plunge the cosmos into darkness. One hears her histrionic exultation in the ecstasy of her high strain of language.

There is a revelatory disconnect between her subsequent ejaculations and Antony's stately assertions of pride. Antony also, despite his death throes, seems to enjoy his own language in: "I am dying, Egypt, dying." When he asks for a final kiss, her melodramatic response again centers upon only her own performance. She seems more interested in the indignity of having to face Octavia's demure stare than in the agony of Antony's death throes. The comic aspects of Antony and Cleopatra enter in her refusal to listen as he speaks his last words:

> **Cleopatra:** Here's sport indeed! How heavy weighs my lord!
> Our strength is all gone into heaviness,
> That makes the weight. Had I great Juno's power,
> The strong-winged Mercury should fetch thee up
> And set thee by Jove's side. Yet come a little;
> Wishes were ever fools. Oh, come, come, come!
> [*They heave Antony aloft to Cleopatra*]
> And welcome, welcome! Die where thou hast lived;
> Quicken with kissing. Had my lips that power,
> Thus would I wear them out.   [*She kisses him*]
> **All:** A heavy sight!
> **Antony:** I am dying, Egypt, dying.
> Give me some wine, and let me speak a little.
> **Cleopatra:** No, let me speak, and let me rail so high
> That the false huswife Fortune break her wheel,
> Provoked by my offence.
>
> act 4, scene 15, lines 33–47

Palpably Cleopatra wishes to enact a final consummation with Antony, the slang meaning of "die," though sadly he can no longer quicken to that fulfillment. Antony or is it Shakespeare delights us by repeating the gorgeous "I am dying, Egypt, dying." Her response is hilarious, denouncing Fortune as a treacherous hussy, while herself shouting like one.

Bungling everything down to the very end, Antony advises her to trust only Proculeius among the captains of Octavius. Proculeius in fact will lie to her and it will be Dolabella who warns her that the victor will lead her in triumph. Shakespeare surges to the heights with Antony's final words and Cleopatra's sublime shock, initially unable to absorb his loss:

> **Antony:** The miserable change now at my end
> Lament nor sorrow at, but please your thoughts
> In feeding them with those my former fortunes,
> Wherein I lived the greatest prince o'th' world,
> The noblest; and do now not basely die,
> Not cowardly put off my helmet to
> My countryman—a Roman by a Roman
> Valiantly vanquished. Now my spirit is going;
> I can no more.
> **Cleopatra:**   Noblest of men, woo't die?
> Hast thou no care of me? Shall I abide
> In this dull world, which in thy absence is
> No better than a sty? [*Antony dies*] Oh, see, my women,
> The crown o'th' earth doth melt. My lord!
> Oh, withered is the garland of the war;
> The soldier's pole is fall'n! Young boys and girls
> Are level now with men. The odds is gone,
> And there is nothing left remarkable
> Beneath the visiting moon.
> [*She faints*]
>
> act 4, scene 15, lines 53–70

Antony, noblest at the close, urges her neither to lament nor to sorrow but to remember his former greatness and the manner of his Roman death, valiantly vanquished only by himself. As he dies, Cleopatra forsakes histrionics and croons her desolation tenderly. She realizes that everyone else bores her and passionately salutes the falling away of his polestar or battle flag and of his sexual strength wasting away in death. Her great outcry "the odds is gone" implies there is no longer a difference between large and small, and there is nothing worth the stakes.

It would be difficult to overpraise this sublime lamentation that is also a high celebration of departed greatness. However grandiose Cleopatra may sound, she is not acting, but is carried up by an exaltation that achieves an ultimate eloquence.

"I shall win at the odds," Hamlet says, going into the death duel with Laertes. He does win and if he dies, that is welcome to him. Hamlet is a universe away from Cleopatra. When she comes out of her swoon, there is a return to the great actress playing her farewells and yet her language is touched by a new nobility:

No more, but e'en a woman, and commanded
By such poor passion as the maid that milks
And does the meanest chares. It were for me
To throw my scepter at the injurious gods,
To tell them that this world did equal theirs
Till they had stol'n our jewel. All's but naught;
Patience is sottish, and impatience does
Become a dog that's mad. Then is it sin
To rush into the secret house of death
Ere death dare come to us? How do you, women?
What, what, good cheer! Why, how now, Charmian?
My noble girls! Ah, women, women! Look,
Our lamp is spent, it's out. Good sirs, take heart.
We'll bury him; and then what's brave, what's noble,
Let's do't after the high Roman fashion

And make death proud to take us. Come, away.
This case of that huge spirit now is cold.
Ah, women, women! Come. We have no friend
But resolution, and the briefest end.

> [*Exeunt; those above bearing off Antony's body*]
> act 4, scene 15, lines 78–96

Rejecting foolish patience and insane impatience as being of
no utility, she asks the rhetorical question of whether it is sinful
for her to precipitate herself into the secret house of death, before
death has the audacity to claim her. Certainly she is again playact-
ing and doubts her own resolution. The high Roman fashion is not
hers, but she will die an Egyptian death.

CHAPTER 12

The Round World /
Should Have Shook Lions
into Civil Streets

Shakespeare grants us an interval between Cleopatra's intense art of dissimulation and her gathering desolation. He centers us entirely upon Octavius Caesar with a portrayal at once dispassionate and chilling. Octavius's incredulous response to the realization that Antony is dead liberates his own dormant capacity for eloquence:

Octavius: The breaking of so great a thing should make
A greater crack. The round world
Should have shook lions into civil streets
And citizens to their dens. The death of Antony
Is not a single doom; in the name lay
A moiety of the world.
Dercetas: He is dead, Caesar,
Not by a public minister of justice,
Nor by a hirèd knife; but that self hand
Which writ his honor in the acts it did

Hath, with the courage which the heart did lend it,
Splitted the heart. This is his sword.   [*He offers the sword*]
I robbed his wound of it. Behold it stained
With his most noble blood.
Octavius: Look you, sad friends?
The gods rebuke me, but it is tidings
To wash the eyes of kings.
Agrippa: And strange it is
That nature must compel us to lament
Our most persisted deeds.
Maecenas: His taints and honors
Waged equal with him.
Agrippa: A rarer spirit never
Did steer humanity; but you gods will give us
Some faults to make us men. Caesar is touched.
Mecaenas: When such a spacious mirror's set before him,
He needs must see himself.

act 5, scene 1, lines 14–35

"Breaking" has a Yeatsian tonality since it comprehends revelation, destruction, and a fresh making of the world. The "crack" is at once a breaking apart and a fearsome clamor. As when Julius Caesar was assassinated, lions should have been unleashed in the city and fleeing citizens should have been running to their own dens or indeed into the lair of the lions. Antony's death is the ruin of many and the restoration of his enemies. Antony's very name held a moiety or half of the universe.

What are we to make of the tears of Octavius Caesar? His yes-men offer qualified praise of the dead Herculean while com-

mending their master for his unlikely tenderness. Octavius again
is moved to an eloquence scarcely in his character:

Octavius:　　　　　　　O Antony,
I have followed thee to this; but we do launch
Diseases in our bodies. I must perforce
Have shown to thee such a declining day,
Or look on thine; we could not stall together
In the whole world. But yet let me lament
With tears as sovereign as the blood of hearts
That thou, my brother, my competitor
In top of all design, my mate in empire,
Friend and companion in the front of war,
The arm of mine own body, and the heart
Where mine his thoughts did kindle—that our stars,
Unreconciliable, should divide
Our equalness to this. Hear me, good friends—　　　[*Enter an*
　　Egyptian]
But I will tell you at some meeter season.
The business of this man looks out of him;
We'll hear him what he says.—Whence are you?
Egyptian: A poor Egyptian yet, the Queen, my mistress,
Confined in all she has, her monument,
Of thy intents desires instruction,
That she preparedly may frame herself
To th' way she's forced to.
Octavius:　　　　　　　Bid her have good heart.
She soon shall know of us, by some of ours,
How honorable and how kindly we

Determine for her. For Caesar cannot live
To be ungentle.

Egyptian: So the gods preserve thee!

act 5, scene 1, lines 35–60

Octavius, moving toward his usual mode, waves aside false regrets and admits he pursued Antony to extinction. Rather dubiously, he asserts the necessity of curing himself by lancing his rival as a disease in his own system. Essentially and accurately he says that it was either you or me. One had to go. Each took up all the space and they could never have dwelt together. He tells us he weeps but we cannot believe him. When he calls Antony his brother, he intends to mean more than brother-in-law yet that is all the truth. "My competitor" is precise: agonist, former partner, equal power monger.

Shakespeare's subtle art informs the move by Octavius to a more deceptive rhetoric. Antony fought at the front of his men; Octavius Caesar safely commanded from the rear. Antony was indeed his sword arm, and the Herculean brave heart served only to kindle thoughts of courage in the canny Octavius. Finally, the stars are blamed for making the two former partners deadly opponents.

He is relieved to break off to hear Cleopatra's messenger and becomes himself again. Needing her treasure to pay his troops and desiring to parade her through the streets of Rome in his triumph, Octavius praises himself for honor, gentleness, and kindness though he is too shrewd not to know she will not believe a word. Her greatness of spirit he acknowledges and rues, and moves to outwit the serpent of old Nile.

Shakespeare concludes this curious negative epiphany of Octavius with the politic future Emperor Augustus going off with his followers to continue self-justification. He pleads his reluctance to pursue Antony and cites his supposed gentle calm in the letters sent to his rival.

Sometimes when I reread this scene I marvel at Shakespeare's reticent control in this portrait of power. Once again what we think of Octavius is left entirely to our own perspective.

CHAPTER 13

He Words Me,
Girls, He Words Me

The pageant of Cleopatra's glorious closing scenes begins with her gradual and necessarily grudging ascent to the apotheosis of her great career:

> **Cleopatra:** My desolation does begin to make
> A better life. 'Tis paltry to be Caesar;
> Not being Fortune, he's but Fortune's knave,
> A minister of her will. And it is great
> To do that thing that ends all other deeds,
> Which shackles accidents and bolts up change,
> Which sleeps and never palates more the dung,
> The beggar's nurse and Caesar's.
>
> act 5, scene 2, lines 1–8

Cleopatra initially takes on the role of a heroine defying Fortune while deprecating Octavius Caesar. He is merely Fortune's servant. Resolving again on suicide, she praises her own greatness in going toward a deep sleep beyond change and accident, and in which she will no longer taste with relish the manure that nurses Octavius and the common beggar.

[*Enter Proculeius*]

Proculeius: Caesar sends greeting to the Queen of Egypt,
And bids thee study on what fair demands
Thou mean'st to have him grant thee.

Cleopatra: What's thy name?

Proculeius: My name is Proculeius.

Cleopatra: Antony
Did tell me of you, bade me trust you; but
I do not greatly care to be deceived
That have no use for trusting. If your master
Would have a queen his beggar, you must tell him
That majesty, to keep decorum, must
No less beg than a kingdom. If he please
To give me conquered Egypt for my son,
He gives me so much of mine own as I
Will kneel to him with thanks.

Proculeius: Be of good cheer;
You're fallen into a princely hand. Fear nothing.
Make your full reference freely to my lord,
Who is so full of grace that it flows over
On all that need. Let me report to him
Your sweet dependency, and you shall find
A conqueror that will pray in aid for kindness
Where he for grace is kneeled to.

Cleopatra: Pray you tell him
I am his fortune's vassal and I send him
The greatness he has got. I hourly learn
A doctrine of obedience, and would gladly
Look him i'th' face.

Proculeius: This I'll report, dear lady.
Have comfort, for I know your plight is pitied
Of him that caused it.

                        act 5, scene 2, lines 9–34

In the dialogue with Proculeius, Cleopatra plays the obedient suppliant but in the barbed language of a bitter irony. Conquered Egypt, though her own, is begged for Caesarion, her son by Julius Caesar, to be garroted at the age of seventeen by the order of Octavius. Grimly she salutes Octavius Caesar by acknowledging "the greatness he has got" by overwhelming force.

[*Roman soldiers enter from behind Cleopatra and take her prisoner*]
Proculeius: [*to the Soldiers*] You see how easily she may be
     surprised.
Guard her till Caesar come.
Iras: Royal Queen!
Charmian: Oh, Cleopatra, thou art taken, Queen.
Cleopatra: Quick, quick, good hands. [*Draws a dagger*]
Proculeius: Hold, worthy lady, hold!
[*Disarms her*] Do not yourself such wrong, who are in this
Relieved, but not betrayed.
Cleopatra: What, of death too,
That rids our dogs of languish?
Proculeius: Cleopatra,
Do not abuse my master's bounty by
Th'undoing of yourself. Let the world see
His nobleness well acted, which your death
Will never let come forth.

Cleopatra: Where art thou, Death?
Come hither, come! Come, come and take a queen
Worth many babes and beggars!

act 5, scene 2, lines 35–47

Surprised by the Roman soldiers who pinion her, she draws her dagger when released, though with so consummate an actress we cannot be certain that she would stab herself if she could. Her marvelous response to the absurdity of Proculeius saying he has rescued and not betrayed her is to cry out that she has been deprived even of death and betrayed of her right to die.

Proculeius: Oh, temperance, lady!
Cleopatra: Sir, I will eat no meat, I'll not drink, sir;
If idle talk will once be necessary,
I'll not sleep, neither. This mortal house I'll ruin,
Do Caesar what he can. Know, sir, that I
Will not wait pinioned at your master's court,
Nor once be chastised with the sober eye
Of dull Octavia. Shall they hoist me up
And show me to the shouting varletry
Of censuring Rome? Rather a ditch in Egypt
Be gentle grave unto me! Rather on Nilus' mud
Lay me stark nak'd, and let the waterflies
Blow me into abhorring! Rather make
My country's high pyramides my gibbet
And hang me up in chains!

act 5, scene 2, lines 47–61

Proculeius is nasty in his sly irony that the nobility of Octavius would not be acted out in his Roman triumph if her death deprived him of her public humiliation. Cleopatra's dramatic art is heard in her fourfold "come" that erotically is addressed to death, urging it to take her, an urgency beyond its too frequent devouring of infants and beggars.

Theatricalism, Cleopatra's genius, is almost too strident as she vows to starve herself of meat, wine, and slumber so as to thwart Octavius Caesar. Her vision of a horror of humiliation awaiting her in Rome evokes the shouting rabblement of plebeians who would exult at her degradation. Beyond all bounds she even pains us with a terrible image of her seductive beauty stark naked in the mud of the Nile, swelled up with maggots as the waterflies make her corpse a depository for their eggs. After that grotesque nightmare, it is almost a relief to see her hung up in chains from a pyramid.

Shakespeare interposes a little ease with the entrance of Dolabella:

Dolabella: Most noble Empress, you have heard of me?
Cleopatra: I cannot tell.
Dolabella: Assuredly you know me.
Cleopatra: No matter, sir, what I have heard or known.
You laugh when boys or women tell their dreams;
Is't not your trick?
Dolabella: I understand not, madam.
Cleopatra: I dreamt there was an emperor Antony.
Oh, such another sleep, that I might see
But such another man!
Dolabella: If it might please ye—

Cleopatra: His face was as the heavens, and therein stuck
A sun and moon which kept their course and lighted
The little O, the earth.

Dolabella: Most sovereign creature—

Cleopatra: His legs bestrid the ocean; his reared arm
Crested the world; his voice was propertied
As all the tunèd spheres, and that to friends;
But when he meant to quail and shake the orb,
He was as rattling thunder. For his bounty,
There was no winter in't; an autumn 'twas
That grew the more by reaping. His delights
Were dolphinlike; they showed his back above
The element they lived in. In his livery
Walked crowns and crownets; realms and islands were
As plates dropped from his pocket.

act 5, scene 2, lines 70–91

There are overtones here of Revelation 10:1–2:

And I saw another mighty Angel come down from heaven, clothed with a cloud, and the rainbow upon his head, and his face was as the sun, and his feet as pillars of fire.

And he had in his hand a little book open, and he put his right foot upon the sea, and *his* left on the earth.

Geneva Bible

This appears to have fused with a passage from the sixteenth-century mythographer Cartari where Jove or Jupiter is identified with the entire universe. Cleopatra's waking dream is of an Antony who is both emperor and god. The intricate web of Cleopatra's guile now extends to a great dream of her lost lover. Antony is transformed into the celestial alternation of sun and moon, lighting our Earth as the little O, the Globe Theatre in which Cleopatra stages her art. Like the Colossus of Rhodes, Antony's legs straddle the ocean. His Herculean arm surmounted the universe and his voice, addressing his followers, brought back the harmony of the heavenly bodies moving in their spheres. But when roaring at his enemies, it shook the world like thunder rattling. His bounty was perpetual harvest and his delight, like dolphins playfully rising up out of the ocean, transcended and gloried in his own being. Kings and princes were his followers, and he strewed countries and islands like so many coins dropping out of his pocket.

Dolabella's courteous dissent spurs Cleopatra to fresh eloquence. Even if such an Antony never existed, mere dreaming cannot dim her image. Shakespeare for once speaks through her: No natural material can compete with fancy or imagination yet his Antony is nature's masterpiece, a triumph over the shadows of stage representation.

Dolabella: Cleopatra—
Cleopatra: Think you there was or might be such a man
As this I dreamt of?
Dolabella: Gentle madam, no.
Cleopatra: You lie up to the hearing of the gods.
But, if there be nor ever were one such,
It's past the size of dreaming. Nature wants stuff
To vie strange forms with fancy; yet t'imagine
An Antony were nature's piece 'gainst fancy,
Condemning shadows quite.

act 5, scene 2, lines 91–99

That is Cleopatra's vision at its highest. Her imagination of Antony surpasses nature, and yet becomes nature's masterpiece.

Dolabella: Hear me, good madam:
Your loss is as yourself, great; and you bear it
As answering to the weight. Would I might never
O'ertake pursued success but I do feel,
By the rebound of yours, a grief that smites
My very heart at root.
Cleopatra: I thank you, sir.
Know you what Caesar means to do with me?
Dolabella: I am loath to tell you what I would you knew.
Cleopatra: Nay, pray you, sir.
Dolabella: Though he be honorable—
Cleopatra: He'll lead me, then, in triumph.
Dolabella: Madam, he will. I know't.

act 5, scene 2, lines 99–109

Moved by her sorrow, Dolabella reveals the intention of Octavius to lead her as the humiliated whore in his Roman celebration. The entrance of Octavius Caesar provokes a tableau both comic and harrowing. Cleopatra grovels and presents him a false scroll of her treasure, calling upon her treasurer Seleucus to verify her. Exposed, she rages and pretends to accept her conqueror's false assurances. When he departs, Cleopatra's resolution becomes firm:

Cleopatra: He words me, girls, he words me, that I should not
Be noble to myself. But hark thee, Charmian.
[*She whispers to Charmian*]
Iras: Finish, good lady. The bright day is done,

And we are for the dark.
Cleopatra: [*to Charmian*] Hie thee again.
I have spoke already and it is provided;
Go put it to the haste.
Charmian: Madam, I will.

                       act 5, scene 2, lines 191–96

There is an ocean of luminous self-realization in Cleopatra's "He words me, girls, he words me." In act 2, scene 2, Hamlet sets the tone:

Polonius: What do you read, my lord?
Hamlet: Words, words, words.

                       act 2, scene 2, lines 188–89

The most restless of intellectuals, Hamlet is impatient not merely with the fussy Polonius but with his own verbal mastery. To unpack his heart with words is to be a drab, or prostitute. One sees why Nietzsche followed Hamlet in the maxim that if you can find words for it, it is already dead in your heart. But Cleopatra as a great diva scorns the deceptions of others and treasures her own labors to deceive. Octavius Caesar is an amateur thespian out of his league when he seeks to entrap an authentic prima donna.

Like her faithful Iras, Cleopatra knows the bright day is done and she is for the dark. With majestic style she goes toward it.

CHAPTER 14

Some Squeaking Cleopatra
Boy My Greatness

Warned by Dolabella that there are only three days at most before Octavius Caesar carries her and her children off to Rome, Cleopatra resolves to perform her final scene:

Cleopatra: Now, Iras, what think'st thou?
Thou an Egyptian puppet shall be shown
In Rome as well as I. Mechanic slaves
With greasy aprons, rules, and hammers shall
Uplift us to the view. In their thick breaths,
Rank of gross diet, shall be enclouded
And forced to drink their vapour.
Iras: The gods forbid!
Cleopatra: Nay, 'tis most certain, Iras. Saucy lictors
Will catch at us like strumpets, and scald rhymers
Ballad us out o' tune. The quick comedians
Extemporally will stage us and present
Our Alexandrian revels; Antony
Shall be brought drunken forth; and I shall see
Some squeaking Cleopatra boy my greatness
I'th' posture of a whore.

Iras: O the good gods!

Cleopatra: Nay, that's certain.

Iras: I'll never see't! For I am sure my nails

Are stronger than mine eyes.

Cleopatra: Why, that's the way

To fool their preparation and to conquer

Their most absurd intents.   [*Enter Charmian*]

               Now, Charmian!

Show me, my women, like a queen. Go fetch

My best attires. I am again for Cydnus,

To meet Mark Antony. Sirrah Iras, go—

Now, noble Charmian, we'll dispatch indeed—

And, when thou hast done this chare I'll give thee leave

To play till doomsday. Bring our crown and all.

               act 5, scene 2, line 207–32

As though directing her own nightmare, Cleopatra with astonishing vividness envisions the potential humiliations of Antony and herself. It would be a puppet show in which slave laborers would raise her up for the delectation of the Roman multitudes. Cleopatra and her women would be all but suffocated by the rank vapors of coarseness and grossness.

The terror augments as Cleopatra describes ribald bailiffs snatching at the Egyptian aristocratic women like so many Doll Tearsheets while scurvy poetlings tunelessly defame them in demotic ballads. Street comedians will exercise their wits in extemporaneous skits featuring an intoxicated Antony. Worst of all, Cleopatra will have to endure a boy actor reducing her greatness to a squeaking harlot.

Shakespeare would have known that women performed upon

the Roman stage. Ruefully he must have chafed at the legal restriction that only boys impersonated his women characters. I've always wondered how even a skilled Jacobean boy actor could have successfully performed the role of Cleopatra.

With forceful pride, the Egyptian queen exults in her preparations to frustrate Octavius Caesar. She wishes to be displayed like an empress. Charmian and Iras are dispatched to bring back her most seductive costume. Once again she will prepare to meet Mark Antony as first she did. As she calls for her crown she utters the uncanny promise that when their chore is performed they can play until doomsday. The arrival of the rural Clown marks the advent of her final epiphany.

Ultimately Cleopatra's staging of her death rivals Hamlet's. He goes into the trap set by Claudius and Laertes fully aware he will not survive. Both Cleopatra and Hamlet die by poison, but that is a limited similarity. What is akin is the appearance of choice in these common fatalities. William Butler Yeats believed that the protagonists of tragedy were beyond sorrow:

All perform their tragic play,
There struts Hamlet, there is Lear,
That's Ophelia, that Cordelia;
Yet they, should the last scene be there,
The great stage curtain about to drop,
If worthy their prominent part in the play,
Do not break up their lines to weep.
They know that Hamlet and Lear are gay;
Gaiety transfiguring all that dread.
All men have aimed at, found and lost;
Black out; Heaven blazing into the head:

Tragedy wrought to its uttermost.
Though Hamlet rambles and Lear rages,
And all the drop scenes drop at once
Upon a hundred thousand stages,
It cannot grow by an inch or an ounce.

"Lapis Lazuli," lines 9–24

In a related, far more splendid poem, Yeats achieved a vision of Homer's Helen that has an aura also of Cleopatra:

That the topless towers be burnt
And men recall that face,
Move most gently if move you must
In this lonely place.
She thinks, part woman, three parts a child,
That nobody looks; her feet
Practise a tinker shuffle
Picked up on a street.
Like a long-legged fly upon the stream
Her mind moves upon silence.

"Long-legged Fly," lines 11–20

One sees the young Cleopatra of Egypt, like the young Helen of Troy, practicing a seductive dance to street musicians, wandering tinkers. Certainly part of the allure of both mythic beauties is the childlike wonder that never abandons them. They know that love is play, however dark it may become.

He. Dear, I must be gone
While night shuts the eyes

Of the household spies;
That song announces dawn.

She. No, night's bird and love's
Bids all true lovers rest,
While his loud song reproves
The murderous stealth of day.

He. Daylight already flies
From mountain crest to crest

She. That light is from the moon.

He. That bird . . .

She. Let him sing on,
I offer to love's play
My dark declivities.
                    "A Woman Young and Old," section VII, "Parting"

This aubade, distantly reminiscent of Romeo and Juliet, is Yeats in the vein of Cleopatra, high priestess of heterosexual love. If Fortune and Octavius Caesar had allowed Antony to survive and Cleopatra to be forever with him, then she would have offered her dark declivities to love's play until doomsday.

CHAPTER 15

I Wish You All Joy
of the Worm

Cleopatra's dialogue with the rural Clown who brings her the fatal asps in a basket of figs is, in one sense, only an interlude before her magnificent self-immolation. And yet when I muse in meditation upon her vast drama, I frequently begin with this curious encounter between incommensurate personalities.

The Clown, like Falstaff's Mistress Quickly, moves from one malapropism to another. Cleopatra, in part amused but increasingly impatient with him, dallies in a last holding off of the darkness:

Guardsman: Here is a rural fellow
That will not be denied Your Highness' presence.
He brings you figs.
Cleopatra: Let him come in.   [*Exit Guardsman*]
          What poor an instrument
May do a noble deed! He brings me liberty.
My resolution's placed, and I have nothing
Of woman in me. Now from head to foot
I am marble-constant; now the fleeting moon
No planet is of mine.
          [*Enter Guardsman and Clown (with a basket)*]

Guardsman: This is the man.

Cleopatra: Avoid, and leave him. [*Exit Guardsman*]

Hast thou the pretty worm of Nilus there

That kills and pains not?

Clown: Truly, I have him, but I would not be the party
that should desire you to touch him, for his biting is
immortal. Those that do die of it do seldom or never
recover.

Cleopatra: Remember'st thou any that have died on't?

Clown: Very many, men and women too. I heard of one of
them no longer than yesterday—a very honest woman,
but something given to lie, as a woman should not do
but in the way of honesty—how she died of the biting of
it, what pain she felt. Truly, she makes a very good report
o'th' worm. But he that will believe all that they say shall
never be saved by half that they do. But this is most
fallible, the worm's an odd worm.

Cleopatra: Get thee hence, farewell.

Clown: I wish you all joy of the worm. [*Sets down his basket*]

act 5, scene 2, lines 233–58

Ironically reflecting that the Clown is a poor instrument that
will enable her to perform the noble deed of suicide, Cleopatra
chills us by terming the poisonous serpents her liberty. We believe
her when she affirms she is fixed in resolution yet wonder why she
wants to assert that she no longer has anything of woman in her.
More than ever, her power is that of female sexuality, an otherness
that even Shakespeare can only intimate. Is she as constant as so
much marble? How can she repudiate the changing moon? Possi-

bly she is aware of her coming transmutation into the goddess Isis, one of whose emblems was the disc of the sun.

The dialogue between Cleopatra and the Clown is fiercely erotic. To call the asp the "pretty worm of Nilus" converts the serpent into the male sexual organ. To be killed without pain is to die in coition.

The Clown, moved by desire for her, warns her not to touch the asp, since its biting is "immortal," by which he means "mortal," yet Shakespeare intends both. The Clown almost matches Cleopatra as a wit when he remarks that those dying by the asp seldom or never recover.

A kind of wonder, outpacing histrionics, moves Cleopatra to the fraught question: "Remember'st thou any that have died on't?" His reply is a little masterpiece of sexual innuendo. Just yesterday he heard from a particular customer, a woman equivocally honest and so given to lie, as only a chaste woman should, who had just died of a bite of the asp and makes a very good report of the worm, thus living on for further erotic forays. In a further turn of travesty, the Clown twists "all" and "half" in distrust of womankind. It would be difficult to refute his malapropism of using "fallible" for "infallible" in asserting that the worm, in every sense, is an odd worm.

Dismissing the Clown, Cleopatra evokes his somewhat bitter "I wish you all joy of the worm." And yet he is not ready to depart:

Cleopatra: Farewell.
Clown: You must think this, look you, that the worm will do his kind.
Cleopatra: Ay, ay; farewell.
Clown: Look you, the worm is not to be trusted but in the

keeping of wise people; for, indeed, there is no goodness
in the worm.

Cleopatra: Take thou no care; it shall be heeded.

Clown: Very good. Give it nothing, I pray you, for it is not
worth the feeding.

Cleopatra: Will it eat me?

Clown: You must not think I am so simple but I know the
devil himself will not eat a woman. I know that a woman
is a dish for the gods, if the devil dress her not. But truly,
these same whoreson devils do the gods great harm in
their women, for in every ten that they make, the devils
mar five.

Cleopatra: Well, get thee gone. Farewell.

Clown: Yes, forsooth. I wish you joy o'th' worm.

act 5, scene 2, lines 259–76

Rather like the aristocratic Dolabella, the rustic is half in love
with her. Warning her again that the worm has no goodness, he
renders Cleopatra more impatient for him to be gone, and still he
lingers to pray her not to die. I often tell my students that her finest moment is when, like a little girl, she asks: "Will it eat me?" In
his exasperation he utters a misogynistic curse, eloquent enough,
though to no purpose. Cleopatra waves him away and he exits
muttering his ambiguous motto "I wish you joy o'th' worm."

When I stand back from this dark dialogue, invariably I recall
Hamlet and the Gravedigger in the first scene of Act 5. In all of
that still amazingly experimental drama, it is only the Gravedigger
who holds his own confronting Hamlet. Digging Ophelia's grave
in consecrated ground, despite her suicide, the saturnine Gravedigger praises his profession as being Adamic.

Hamlet and Horatio enter just as the Gravedigger throws up the skull of Yorick, jester to the murdered King Hamlet, and a loving playmate to the child Hamlet. The emblem of *The Tragical History of Hamlet, Prince of Denmark* is Hamlet holding up and confronting Yorick's skull. Certainly one emblem of *The Tragedy of Antony and Cleopatra* is the Queen of Egypt raising the asps to her breast and to her arm.

The Gravedigger is far more formidable than the Clown. His equivocations are equal to Hamlet's deep questionings and endless dole. One could say his earthy realism sets off Hamlet's supernal nihilism. Cleopatra's embodiment of the moist soil and water of the Nile will be cast away by her as she ascends to what she hopes yet will be a transcendent reunion with her lost lover.

CHAPTER 16

I Am Fire and Air

Shakespeare, as we might expect, has unique mastery at portraying the art of dying. We do not see Sir John Falstaff die. That is as it should be. It is good to remember him counterfeiting death on the battlefield and then resurrecting in the fullness of his glory. Mistress Quickly, tenderly and falteringly, croons her prose elegy for the Fat Knight.

Hamlet dies onstage and mysteriously frustrates us by saying that if there were time, he would tell us, and we will never know what that would have been. His last words are enigmatic: "The rest is silence." Does "rest" mean "remainder" or does it imply perpetual peace? My mentor Gershom Scholem and his tragic friend Walter Benjamin believed that speech was marred in the Creation-Fall while silence remained unblemished.

Though the warrior Fortinbras awards Hamlet military honors for his funeral, we tolerate this irony because he commands Hamlet to be carried up to a high place, and that elevation gratifies our sense that the Prince of Denmark has died upward onto a supernal plane.

King Lear, the great image of paternal and royal authority, dies in the beautiful delusion that his daughter Cordelia has been resurrected, and that onrush of joy breaks his overstrained heart. His friend Gloucester similarly ends betwixt joy and grief, as narrated to us by Edgar, his legitimate son and heir. Edmund the Bastard, his natural all-too-natural son, is carried off stage to die after being cut down by Edgar. We do not see the terrible death of Cordelia, strangled by Edmund's order, though her furious father, despite being well on in his eighties, destroys her murderer.

The monster daughters of Lear, Goneril and Regan, die off-stage, and their bodies are then carried in. Goneril has poisoned Regan and then killed herself. The Fool vanishes and we do not know where or why.

We see the deaths both of Desdemona, strangled by Othello, and then of the Moor, who stabs himself in expiation. Emilia is slain onstage by her infuriated husband, Iago, who then vows silence, knowing he will die under torture.

Lady Macbeth, in her madness, evidently is a suicide. Macbeth, Shakespeare's ultimate hero-villain, is slain offstage by Macduff, who enters brandishing the tyrant's head. Perhaps we do not see Macbeth die because Shakespeare has compelled us to travel so far into the interior with Bellona's bridegroom that we cannot help identifying with him.

That tragic Shakespearean procession has no particular pattern that I can discern. I cite it here to suggest the enormous contrast of all these with the high artistry Cleopatra brings to her earthly conclusion. We have seen Antony's pathetic death, a painful decline from his Herculean splendor. Cleopatra chooses to die upward in an audacious venture into the Elysian Fields. If she has any affinity with the Shakespearean personalities who have preceded her, I can think only of Hamlet, but he chooses to die into nothingness.

Cleopatra's histrionic consciousness mounts to a summit with majestic language:

[*Enter Iras with a robe, crown and other jewels*]

Cleopatra: Give me my robe. Put on my crown. I have

Immortal longings in me. Now no more

The juice of Egypt's grape shall moist this lip.

[*The women dress her*]

Yare, yare, good Iras; quick. Methinks I hear

Antony call; I see him rouse himself

To praise my noble act. I hear him mock

The luck of Caesar, which the gods give men

To excuse their after wrath. Husband, I come!

Now to that name my courage prove my title!

I am fire and air; my other elements

I give to baser life. So, have you done?

Come, then, and take the last warmth of my lips.

Farewell, kind Charmian. Iras, long farewell.

        [*Kisses them. Iras falls and dies.*]

Have I the aspic in my lips? Dost fall?

If thou and nature can so gently part,

The stroke of death is as a lover's pinch,

Which hurts and is desired. Dost thou lie still?

If thus thou vanishest, thou tell'st the world

It is not worth leave-taking.

Charmian: Dissolve, thick cloud, and rain, that I may say

The gods themselves do weep!

        act 5, scene 2, lines 277–97

Her immortal longings are not so much for a time without boundaries but for a perpetual fulfillment of her sexual richness and power. As Charmian and Iras dress her, she urges celerity, and imagines Antony calling to praise her nobility, and to mock the fortunes of Octavius Caesar, as though the gods have made Octavius lucky so that at last they can punish him for his pride.

It is startling and wonderful to hear her cry out "Husband, I come!" Her courage must prove her legitimacy as Antony's bride. Fulvia and Octavia are at last exorcised. The tide of her being flows exuberantly as she proclaims:

> I am fire and air; my other elements
> I give to baser life.

Fully attired, she turns to kiss farewell to Charmian and to Iras, who expires immediately by that kiss of death. In wonderment, Cleopatra ironically asks if the poison of the asp is already in her lips. She is altogether herself when she muses:

> If thou and nature can so gently part,
> The stroke of death is as a lover's pinch,
> Which hurts and is desired.

Dying is erotic play and gentle Iras has vanished without the ceremony of farewell. Cleopatra, more than ever, is ceremonial while Charmian weeps with the gods of Egypt. And so Cleopatra begins the sacrament of her departure:

Cleopatra: This proves me base.
If she first meet the curlèd Antony,
He'll make demand of her, and spend that kiss
Which is my heaven to have. [*To an asp*] Come, thou mortal
    wretch,

With thy sharp teeth this knot intrinsicate
Of life at once untie. Poor venomous fool,
Be angry and dispatch. Oh, couldst thou speak,
That I might hear thee call great Caesar ass
Unpolicied!
Charmian: O eastern star!
Cleopatra: Peace, peace!
Dost thou not see my baby at my breast,
That sucks the nurse asleep?
Charmian: Oh, break! Oh, break!
Cleopatra: As sweet as balm, as soft as air, as gentle—
O Antony!—Nay, I will take thee too.
                    [*Applies another asp to her arm*]
What should I stay—   [*Dies*]
                    act 5, scene 2, lines 297–310

She hastens lest Iras first meet Antony in the Elysian Fields
and request the pleasure of a kiss that would be heaven for the
Egyptian queen. She takes up an asp and affectionately terms it a
deadly beloved. The intricate knot tying her to life she yields up to
the phallic bite of the serpent. Angrily ironic, she wishes the asp to
speak, that it might call Octavius Caesar an outwitted ass, with an
obvious play upon asp.

Charmian, overcome by love and sorrow, magnificently cries out
"O eastern star!" invoking the morning star, Venus, and the memory of Cleopatra's first appearance to Antony in the costume of
that goddess. In an ecstasy, Cleopatra hushes Charmian. As the
poison seeps in, the Egyptian queen identifies the asp with one of
the babies she had nursed and falls asleep even as the infant did.
In Charmian's desperate injunction:

Oh, break! Oh, break!

there is an echo of Kent, faithful follower of King Lear, urging the bereaved old man (or more likely, himself) to escape further torment:

Break, heart; I prithee, break!

act 5, scene 3, line 309

In her final ecstasy, Cleopatra hallucinates that she takes Antony:

As sweet as balm, as soft as air, as gentle—
O Antony!—Nay, I will take thee too.

[*Applies another asp to her arm*]

What should I stay—   [*Dies*]

We will never know how those final words would have concluded. Why should she stay? Charmian answers for her and then follows:

Charmian: In this wild world? So, fare thee well.
Now boast thee, Death, in thy possession lies
A lass unparalleled. Downy windows, close;
And golden Phoebus never be beheld
Of eyes again so royal! Your crown's awry;
I'll mend it, and then play—   [*Enter the Guard, rustling in*]
First Guard: Where's the Queen?
Charmian: Speak softly. Wake her not.
First Guard: Caesar hath sent—
Charmian: Too slow a messenger.

[*She applies an asp to herself*]

Oh, come apace, dispatch! I partly feel thee.

First Guard: Approach, ho! All's not well. Caesar's beguiled.

Second Guard: There's Dolabella sent from Caesar. Call him.

First Guard: What work is here, Charmian? Is this well done?

Charmian: It is well done, and fitting for a princess

Descended of so many royal kings.

Ah, soldier!   [*Charmian dies*]

                  act 5, scene 2, lines 311–25

Charmian appears to mean both a savage and a vile world that is better abandoned. She closes the soft eyebrows of her Queen, and straightens Cleopatra's crown. Quite wonderfully she begins her suicide by calling it "play." A bawdy personality throughout, she dies with the wistful "Ah, soldier!" as though she wants a final embrace.

The death of Cleopatra has been so awesome that we do it violence unless we apprehend how majestic it is. Octavius Caesar enters for a kind of epilogue, but I will postpone that until I consider Cleopatra in the larger context of Shakespeare's pilgrimage through eros.

Falstaff and his companions, Doll Tearsheet and Mistress Quickly in particular, are rammed with life. Their exuberance encircles the erotic sphere of desire and its fulfillment. Defying age and the state, Sir John Falstaff must lose, and yet his passion holds on until the end. In his personality we can surmise a vitalism that Shakespeare both augmented and endorsed.

The Sonnets are too varied for any single pattern, but they move toward the sexual furnace of the Dark Lady. Hamlet, though he insists he loved Ophelia, savagely rejects her in what seems a recoiling from sexuality itself. His contempt for his mother, Gertrude, is painful for us, and difficult to forgive. To say that there shall be no more marriages is the cry of a mistaken soul. Since Hamlet, like his creator, has the most capacious of intelligences, we are moved to woe and wonder by this extremity.

King Lear, furious and crazed by the ingratitude of Goneril and Regan, denounces the vagina as the infernal pit, yet is large enough to be disgusted by his own sourness. Edgar, whose personality is complex beyond comprehension, humbles himself by telling the dying Edmund:

> The gods are just, and of our pleasant vices
> Make instruments to plague us:
> The dark and vicious place where thee he got
> Cost him his eyes.
>
> act 5, scene 3, lines 167–70

We wince, as Edgar does also, that the vagina of Edmund's unknown mother should so be characterized. Where Shakespeare himself stands in this, we have no clue. And yet the plays show us an increasing diffidence, in the older sense of distrustfulness, in regard to the undifferentiated male sex drive.

Iago's bitter language about human sexuality may indicate that the shock of being rejected by Othello has unmanned him. Despite the radiance of Desdemona and the doughty spirit of Emilia, Iago so scatters and ruins Othello that the heroic Moor is reduced to a sexual obsessive.

There are hints that Macbeth is not altogether sexually adequate as the husband of the formidable Lady Macbeth. From 1601 to 1605 Shakespeare composed the three problematic comedies: *Troilus and Cressida, All's Well That Ends Well,* and *Measure for Measure.* After that came the tragic sequence of *Othello, King Lear, Macbeth,* and *Antony and Cleopatra.*

The dark comedies are feculent. Cressida and Helen of Troy pragmatically are whores. *All's Well That Ends Well* and *Measure for Measure* both feature the bed-trick, in which one woman substitutes for another, on the principle that in the dark they are all alike. After the sublimity of Cleopatra, the remaining tragedies are diminishments. In *Coriolanus* the dread figure Volumnia is the archetypal Devouring Mother whose motto is "Anger's my meat." In *Timon of Athens* the protagonist loads with gold the whores Phrynia and Timandra, who accompany Alcibiades on his expedition. Timon commissions these brazen damozels to carry their diseases to the Athenians and thus freely to decimate the ungrateful city.

In the beautiful late romances *The Winter's Tale* and *The Tempest,* Shakespeare returns to his more customary balance. In *The Winter's Tale,* Leontes, overcome by paranoid jealousy, chants his madness:

> It is a bawdy planet, that will strike
> Where 'tis predominant; and 'tis powerful, think it,
> From east, west, north and south: be it concluded,
> No barricado for a belly; know't;
> It will let in and out the enemy
> With bag and baggage: many thousand on's
> Have the disease, and feel't not.
>
> act 1, scene 2, lines 201–7

Against this Shakespeare sets his most convincing and exquisite passage between lovers when Perdita addresses Florizel:

Perdita: Now, my fair'st friend,
I would I had some flowers o' the spring that might
Become your time of day; and yours, and yours,
That wear upon your virgin branches yet
Your maidenheads growing: O Proserpina,
For the flowers now, that frighted thou let'st fall
From Dis's waggon! daffodils,
That come before the swallow dares, and take
The winds of March with beauty; violets dim,
But sweeter than the lids of Juno's eyes
Or Cytherea's breath; pale primroses
That die unmarried, ere they can behold
Bright Phoebus in his strength—a malady
Most incident to maids; bold oxlips and
The crown imperial; lilies of all kinds,
The flower-de-luce being one! O, these I lack,
To make you garlands of, and my sweet friend,
To strew him o'er and o'er!
Florizel: What, like a corse?
Perdita: No, like a bank for love to lie and play on;
Not like a corse; or if, not to be buried,
But quick and in mine arms. Come, take your flowers:
Methinks I play as I have seen them do
In Whitsun pastorals: sure this robe of mine
Does change my disposition.
Florizel: What you do
Still betters what is done. When you speak, sweet.
I'ld have you do it ever: when you sing,
I'ld have you buy and sell so, so give alms,

Pray so; and, for the ordering your affairs,
To sing them too: when you do dance, I wish you
A wave o' the sea, that you might ever do
Nothing but that; move still, still so,
And own no other function: each your doing,
So singular in each particular,
Crowns what you are doing in the present deed,
That all your acts are queens.

act 4, scene 4, lines 112–46

At eighty-six this still moves me to tears. Memories flood me of ecstatic moments more than sixty years ago when love fell upon one. It would be good if this and the love between Miranda and Ferdinand in *The Tempest* had been Shakespeare's final vision of an erotic ideal. Instead, in his final work for the stage, *The Two Noble Kinsmen*, done in collaboration with John Fletcher, Shakespeare horrifies me with the dreadful spectacle of incessant male lust prolonged into grotesquerie:

Palamon: I knew a man
Of eighty winters—this I told them—who
A lass of fourteen brided. 'Twas thy power
To put life into dust: the aged cramp
Had screw'd his square foot round,
The gout had knit his fingers into knots,
Torturing convulsions from his globy eyes
Had almost drawn their spheres, that what was life
In him seem'd torture. This anatomy
Had by his young fair fere a boy, and I

Believ'd it was his, for she swore it was,
And who would not believe her?

act 5, scene 1, lines 107–18

This is from a prayer to the power of Venus. Shakespeare shocks and moves me to silence. It was a long descent from the glory of Cleopatra to this nightmare.

Subdued, I return to the closing movement of *Antony and Cleopatra*. Octavius Caesar is cold and triumphant and yet Shakespeare allows him a moment almost beyond eloquence:

> Oh, noble weakness!
> If they had swallowed poison, 'twould appear
> By external swelling; but she looks like sleep,
> As she would catch another Antony
> In her strong toil of grace.

act 5, scene 2, lines 343–47

"Toil" takes the archaic meaning of "net." Her toil has been strong enough to seduce us and many before and after.

We can wave aside the final speech of Octavius Caesar, in which he compliments himself on his glory in having brought down so famous a pair as Antony and Cleopatra. He promises a mutual burial with military honors. The irony recalls Fortinbras according the same to Hamlet. It is as though Shakespeare, both with Hamlet and with Cleopatra, trusts us to apprehend ironies almost too large to be seen.

ABOUT THE AUTHOR

Harold Bloom is Sterling Professor of Humanities at Yale University and a former Charles Eliot Norton Professor at Harvard. His more than forty books include *The Anxiety of Influence*, *The Western Canon*, *Shakespeare: The Invention of the Human*, *The American Religion*, *How to Read and Why*, *Stories and Poems for Extremely Intelligent Children of All Ages*, and *The Daemon Knows*. He is a member of the American Academy of Arts and Letters, a MacArthur Fellow, and the recipient of many awards and honorary degrees, including the American Academy's Gold Medal for Belles Lettres and Criticism, the Hans Christian Andersen Award, the Catalonia International Prize, and the Alfonso Reyes International Prize of Mexico.